DREAM INTERPRETATION REVEALED

EXPLORE THE SPIRITUAL MEANING OF DREAMS, DECODE SYMBOLS, TRANSFORM NIGHTMARES INTO INSIGHT, & UNLOCK PERSONAL GROWTH THROUGH YOUR SUBCONSCIOUS

M. SALLIE

Copyright © 2025 by M. Sallie

All rights reserved. No part of this publication may be reproduced, distributed, stored in a retrieval system, or transmitted in any form or by any means—electronic, mechanical, photocopying, recording, scanning, or otherwise—without the prior written permission of the author or publisher, except in the case of brief quotations embodied in critical reviews, academic works, or articles, provided full attribution is given.

This book is published by **Ember & Flow Collective**, an independent imprint dedicated to work that supports personal healing, self-discovery, and transformational growth.

First Edition: 2025

Cover design by *didiwahyudi.trend*

This publication is intended for informational, educational, and entertainment purposes only. It does not constitute professional medical, psychological, therapeutic, or legal advice. The author and publisher make no representations or warranties concerning the accuracy or applicability of the content contained in this book.

Do not interpret any reference to specific health practices, including but not limited to vitamins, supplements, dietary routines, or somatic therapies, as medical advice or a substitute for consultation with licensed healthcare providers. Always seek guidance from a qualified medical or mental health professional before changing your health, wellness, or treatment regimen.

Neither the author nor the publisher shall be held liable for any loss, damage, or injury allegedly arising from any information or suggestion in this book.

All characters, stories, and personal experiences described herein are either the product of the author's imagination, used with permission, or adapted to protect confidentiality. Any resemblance to actual persons, living or dead, is purely coincidental unless otherwise stated.

Printed in the United States of America

CONTENTS

Introduction	7
1. DREAM INTERPRETATION REVEALED	13
A Childhood Dream of Flight	13
The Language of Dreams and the Subconscious	14
The Science of Dreams: REM Sleep Unveiled	15
Symbolism of Flying Dreams	16
Looking Ahead	19
2. ENHANCING DREAM RECALL	21
Waking Up with Your Dreams	21
Neurobiology of Dream Memory	22
Why Dream Recall Matters Across Cultures	23
Cultivating Dream Recall	25
Embracing REM Sleep	29
3. BREAKING DOWN DREAM SYMBOLS: COMMON SYMBOLS AND THEIR MEANINGS	31
Common Dream Symbols	34
Exploring Symbols Across Cultures	37
Indigenous Traditions	39
Eastern Traditions	40
African & Latin American Traditions	42
4. ADVANCED DREAM SYMBOLISM	45
Unlocking Archetypes: Carl Jung and Practical Interpretation	48
The Cultural Layer: Archetypes We Inherit	54
Blending the Personal and the Cultural: A Depth-Oriented Approach to Dream Symbolism	57
Blending the Personal and the Cultural: A Depth-Oriented Approach to Dream Symbolism	60
Long-Term Dream Patterns and Life Transitions	61
5. THE ART OF LUCID DREAMING	66
The Magic of Lucid Dreaming	66
Staying in the Dream	72

13. SHARING DREAMS AND GROUP INTERPRETATION 159
    Understanding Dreams Throughout History: Approaches to
    Communal Dream-Sharing
    Then and Now: How Modern Dream Circles Echo
    Ancient Wisdom
    How to Start Your Own Dream Circle (Online or In-
    Person)
    Facilitating Dream Sharing and Group Interpretation
    The Dream That Connects Us All

14. DREAM EXPLORATION FOR CHILDREN
    Why Children Dream Differently
    How to Help a Child Recall and Share Dreams
    Turning Nightmares into Playful Stories
    The Healing Power of Being Heard

INTRODUCTION

When I was nine, my brother, nearly fifteen, vibrant, and always in motion, left us in a heartbeat. He was the spark in our family, dragging me outside to chase the wind or daring me to climb higher than I thought I could. Athletic and fearless, he made everything a game, his grin wide as he'd nudge me forward, saying, "Come on, you can do it; don't wimp out now!" I'd roll my eyes, but secretly, I thrived on it, his belief in me, the way he turned my hesitations into adventures. Our parents would watch from the porch, Mom calling out half-hearted warnings while Dad chuckled, proud of the wild streak we shared. Back then, our house buzzed with noise: laughter, arguments, the clatter of life, and he was at the heart of it.

Then he was gone, and the silence crept in. The family shifted, like a puzzle missing its loudest piece. My parents tried to keep things steady, their love a quiet anchor, but I'd catch Mom staring out the window too long or Dad tinkering in the garage with tools he didn't need. I'd retreat to my brother's room, a time capsule of his world, faded posters curling at the edges, a football still scuffed from our backyard games, the faint whiff of his cologne clinging to the air. It was my refuge, a place to feel him near me. Years later, when my parents decided I should move into that room, it felt both right and wrong. The first night, I lay in his bed, the familiar creak of the frame beneath me, rain tapping softly outside. I could almost hear his voice, teasing me about something silly, and I drifted off with that thought, aching for the comfort it used to bring.

It wasn't long after I moved into his room that the dreams began.

At first, the dreams were quiet, just the sound of rain. Soft, steady, almost comforting. But over time, the rain got louder. It felt heavier somehow, like it wasn't just the weather, but a warning. In the dream, I'd be standing in a street or yard that felt familiar, but wrong in some indescribable way. Water would start rising around my ankles; cold, creeping, unstoppable.

Then it would surge.

The flood would come rushing in, pulling me off balance. I'd try to run, but the current would seize me, hurling me toward a huge storm drain; dark, deep, and roaring like it could rip the ground open beneath me. It made this horrible, sucking roar like it was alive, like it wanted to pull everything under. I'd fight it with everything I had, grabbing at tree roots, fence posts, anything to anchor myself. But nothing held. The water was too strong. The dream always ended the same way: me on the edge, inches from falling in, heart pounding so hard I thought it might burst.

Then I would wake up. Gasping. Soaked in sweat. My sheets twisted around me like I'd been wrestling with something all night.

The nightmare came again and again. For almost two years, it returned in some form; sometimes exactly the same, sometimes shifted just slightly. Always the flood. Always the drain. Always the panic. I never really knew when it would come, and I never understood why I couldn't outrun it. It felt like I was being dragged toward something I wasn't ready to face.

But then, slowly, something changed.

One night, I didn't go under. I grabbed hold of something; maybe a railing, maybe a tree, and it held. I didn't get swept away. The dream still shook me, but I didn't feel powerless in the same way. A few weeks later, it came again, but this time I was already bracing. Already prepared. I knew where the current would come from. I planted my feet. I fought.

Eventually, the dream just stopped!

I can't say exactly why or when. But looking back, I think it marked something in me; a shift from drowning in fear to learning how to meet it. It didn't feel like a lesson at the time. It just felt like survival. But now I wonder if that nightmare was my mind's way of showing me what I didn't know how to process while awake: that the storm wasn't just outside of me. It was inside. And somehow, I had found a way to hold my ground.

As I grew older, the vivid dreams kept coming. They weren't all as terrifying as that childhood nightmare, but many carried the same strange power. In my teens, I often dreamed of being trapped in an endless building, wandering through dim hallways and locked doors, searching desperately for an exit that never appeared. Other nights, I'd step into an elevator that would get stuck between floors or loop me back to the wrong floor no matter how many buttons I pressed. I'd wake from these dreams with a racing heart, disoriented, sometimes even clenching my jaw from the tension. There was always a pattern: *in my dreams, I was stuck, lost, or caught in a loop*, and I woke up feeling the echo of that helplessness. These nocturnal adventures were bizarre and unsettling, yet strangely fascinating. *Why was my subconscious staging these elaborate traps for me? What was I running from–or maybe what was I being pushed toward?*

In college, I finally confronted my curiosity about dreams head-on. Instead of simply being relieved when a nightmare ended, I wanted to understand *why* it began in the first place. I bought a blank journal and started scribbling down every dream I could remember each morning, no matter how fragmented or absurd. At night, I read everything I could find about dream interpretation, from spiritual perspectives to psychology. I even dabbled in lucid dreaming techniques, training myself to realize that I could explore those eerie halls and elevators with more courage when I was dreaming. The deeper I dove, the more it became clear that my dreams, even the scariest ones, held meaning. They were like mirrors reflecting my hidden fears and hopes, or letters from my soul written in symbolic language. The dream of the storm drain, for example, revealed itself not as a random childhood terror but perhaps as my mind's way of processing the overwhelming grief and *storm* of losing my brother. This realization was a turning point. I realized maybe, just maybe, our nightmares could be more than horror shows; they could be guides, offering insight once we learn how to read them.

Over the years, what started as a frightened child's question, *"Why am I dreaming this?"* grew into a lifelong fascination and a calling. I became someone who listens intently to the stories my subconscious tells. Each dream, whether delightful or dreadful, has become an invitation to learn more about myself. In the pages that follow, I'll share some of the most profound dream experiences I've had and what I've discovered from them. My journey has taught me that understanding our dreams can be a powerful tool for healing and personal growth. I've seen nightmares that once tormented me transform into sources of insight and even comfort once I understood their language.

So, dear reader, as you hold this book, I invite you into the world of dreams, your dreams. I invite you to walk with me through the rainstorms of the subconscious and come out the other side stronger. This isn't a dry academic study or a collection of one-size-fits-all interpretations, but a heartfelt conversation and exploration. Think of it as two friends trading stories late into the night, trying to make sense of the images dancing behind our eyelids. I suspect you, too, have had nights of peaceful rains and swirling storms. You, too, carry unforgettable dream memories that feel like keys without locks. Together, let's shine a warm light on those dark dream corners and see what they have to reveal. After all, our dreams, even the nightmares, are part of our story, and understanding them can help us heal, grow, and awaken to a richer life.

Every dream story in this book is my own. What you'll read came from the pages of my personal journal: actual dreams, genuine emotions, and the interpretations I explored through curiosity, intuition, and research. I hope that by sharing them, you'll feel encouraged to listen more deeply to your own.

1

DREAM INTERPRETATION REVEALED

A CHILDHOOD DREAM OF FLIGHT

I still remember the first time I flew. I was about twelve years old, curled up in my bed, when I found myself in a vivid dream running through an open field behind our house. As I picked up speed, the ground suddenly fell away beneath me. I was airborne! The sensation was incredible, the wind brushing past my cheeks, the world below getting smaller. In that childhood dream of flying, I felt pure joy and freedom. There were no limits, no gravity pulling me down, just an overwhelming sense that I could go anywhere.

When I woke up, I lay there for a moment, smiling and wishing I could return to that sky. Even as a child, I sensed something special about that dream, though I didn't yet understand why it moved me so deeply.

That flying dream stayed with me for years. At the time, I thought it was the coolest dream ever, a fun nighttime adventure. But as I grew older, I wondered if it meant more.

Have you ever had a dream that felt so real and meaningful that you couldn't shake it the next day? Many of us have experienced dreams like that, dreams that leave an emotional imprint. My childhood flight was one of those. Looking back now, I realize the dream was my first little window into the world of dream interpretation. It sparked questions in my young mind: *Why did I dream of flying? Was my mind trying to tell me something?* Those questions eventually led me to discover a passion for understanding dreams and the messages they carry.

THE LANGUAGE OF DREAMS AND THE SUBCONSCIOUS

Dreams have a unique way of speaking to us. They don't use words or straightforward logic like our waking minds. Instead, they communicate in symbols, emotions, and scenes. This is the language of our *subconscious mind* at work. Think of the subconscious as a vast ocean beneath the surface of our awareness; it's where our hidden thoughts, feelings, memories, and desires swim quietly, even while we're awake. When we fall asleep, that subconscious ocean waves up to the surface, bringing those hidden pieces of ourselves into the light of our dreams.

Psychologists have long suggested that our dreams are reflections of our innermost thoughts. Sigmund Freud famously said that *"the interpretation of dreams is the royal road to a knowledge of the unconscious activities of the mind"*. By this, he meant that if we examine our dreams, we can learn about the parts of ourselves that we might not be fully aware of when awake. In simpler terms, our dreams are messages from our subconscious, wrapped in imagery and metaphor. If we learn to decode those messages, we gain insight into our feelings and experiences at a deeper level.

Consider how often dream images relate to our lives. If you're feeling anxious about a new job, you might dream you're standing on stage forgetting your lines. If you're proud and happy, you might dream of sunshine, colorful scenes, or, as in my case, soaring through the sky.

These images aren't random; they're your mind's creative way of expressing your feelings, thoughts, or needs. Our conscious mind (the part we think with during the day) might ignore or suppress certain emotions, but the subconscious doesn't hold back. It uses dreams to say, *"Here's how I really feel!"* Understanding this helps explain why that childhood flying dream felt so powerful; some part of me, beyond logic, was speaking through the language of the dream.

THE SCIENCE OF DREAMS: REM SLEEP UNVEILED

While dreams can feel mystical or deeply personal, there's also solid science behind how and when they occur. Most dreaming happens during a stage of sleep known as REM (Rapid Eye Movement) sleep. In REM sleep, our brains are incredibly active; almost as active as when we're awake, yet our bodies are largely paralyzed, so we don't act out our dreams. (Isn't it amazing that you can be flying or running in a dream, but in reality you're safely lying in bed?) This stage is called "Rapid Eye Movement" because your eyes actually dart back and forth beneath your closed eyelids, as if you're watching your dream unfold.

We typically enter our first REM phase about 60 to 90 minutes after falling asleep, and then cycle through REM multiple times in the night. Each cycle of REM can last longer than the previous one, which is why dreams often get more numerous or vivid toward the early morning hours. So, that magical flight I took as a child most likely happened during one of these REM cycles. My brain was lit up with activity, concocting an adventure, while my body stayed still.

What's truly fascinating is *why* the brain creates these dream stories at all. Researchers have found that REM sleep is not just important for dreaming, but also for processing emotions and memories. In fact, during REM sleep, the emotional center of our brain (the amygdala) is especially active. This suggests that dreaming might be a way our minds work through feelings.

Have you ever noticed that you might have intense dreams after a bad day? That's your brain doing overnight therapy; taking the difficulties of the day and playing them out in symbolic form. So, when I dreamt of flying as a kid, perhaps my brain was helping me *feel* free and joyful, especially if I needed those emotions at the time.

Understanding the science of REM sleep gives us a pleasant background: it tells us *when* and *how* dreams happen. But science can't fully explain the personal meaning behind a dream. For that, we turn back to interpretation and the heart.

SYMBOLISM OF FLYING DREAMS

Let's return to that childhood dream of flying. Why is it that soaring through the sky felt so exhilarating and stuck in my memory? As it turns out, I'm far from alone in having flying dreams. People all over the world report dreams of taking flight. These dreams are often delightful and liberating and dream experts believe they carry important symbolism.

Flying in a dream is associated with a sense of freedom and release. Think about it: when you fly, you're literally rising above the ground and leaving restrictions behind. Many modern analyses link dreams of flying with a yearning to break free of limitations in life. It might reflect that you are overcoming something that once held you down or wish to overcome it. In my case, as an imaginative child, floating above the treetops might have been my mind's way of escaping the ordinary and discovering confidence. Indeed, renowned psychologist Carl Jung believed that when a person dreams of rising above the earth, it's because in waking life they may feel weighed down by everyday problems, and the dream is the psyche's way of restoring balance by lifting them up. In other words, my mind might have given me wings in the dream because, deep down, I needed to feel *capable* and *unburdened*.

Flying dreams can carry other positive meanings, too. Sometimes, they signify gaining a new *perspective*. When you're high up in the air, you can see the big picture that's hard to notice on the ground. Similarly, a flying dream can be a sign that you're ready to see your life in a broader way, rising above petty troubles and focusing on what really matters. These dreams can also be about *empowerment*. Feeling joyful and in control while flying might mean you're growing more confident in real life, taking charge of your direction. You might even *cele-*

brate a personal victory or a newfound control over your circumstances.

On the other hand, it's worth noting that the emotions you feel while flying in a dream matter to the interpretation. My childhood flight overjoyed me, pointing to uplifting meanings like freedom and happiness. But if someone feels fear while flying in a dream, perhaps afraid of falling, it could indicate that even though they crave freedom, they also fear the risks that come with it. (Think of the legend of Icarus flying too close to the sun.) However, in this chapter, we're focusing on the uplifting side of flying dreams, because my experience was so positive and illuminating.

To summarize, some key symbolic meanings that flying dreams often represent:

- **Freedom and Independence:** Feeling unchained and liberated, breaking away from everyday limitations. Flying can reflect a desire for personal freedom or a recent sense of *empowerment* and confidence blossoming in your life.
- **Rising Above Challenges:** Soaring above obstacles or stress, showing that you have the ability to overcome difficulties and rise above what's bothering you. It's your mind's way of saying, *"You can handle this—look, you're literally above it!"*
- **Perspective and Control:** Gaining a higher vantage point on your life. You might see things more clearly or taking control, guiding your own path from up high. This often comes with a feeling of clarity, like you're viewing your world in its entirety and understanding where you want to go.

When I learned about these symbolic meanings, it gave my childhood dream even more significance. I realized little me wasn't just having fun at night; my subconscious was gifting me a feeling of freedom, strength, and hope. That understanding filled me with gratitude and excitement. And it also made me eager to pay closer attention to other dreams, because who knew what other insights were waiting up there in the clouds of sleep?

Keeping a Dream Journal: Your Personal Key

By now, you might wonder, *"How can I start understanding my own dreams better?"* One of the most practical and rewarding ways to do that is by keeping a **dream journal**. This is a simple notebook (or an app, if you prefer) where you record what you dream about each night. It might seem straightforward, but it's a powerful tool for unlocking the meanings of your dreams.

Why keep a journal? For one, dreams are notoriously easy to forget. How many times have you woken up with a head full of images, only to have them fade away by breakfast? Writing them down quickly helps capture those delicate memories before they slip. More importantly, a journal lets you see patterns. When you look back after a few weeks, you might notice recurring themes or symbols (maybe you'll dream of flying, teeth falling out, or being late to class; whatever it is, patterns tell a story). It's your subconscious leaving a trail of breadcrumbs, and the journal helps you follow the trail.

I invite you to start your own dream journal as we progress on this journey. Here's a simple exercise to get you started:

1. **Set the Intention (Prepare):** Before you go to bed tonight, place a notebook and pen by your bedside (or have a voice recorder app ready on your phone). Tell yourself, *"I will remember my dream when I wake up."* This intention-setting actually makes it more likely that you *will* remember your dream.
2. **Record Immediately:** When you wake up (whether in the middle of the night or in the morning), avoid jumping out of bed right away. Stay still for a moment and try to replay the dream in your mind. Then, grab your journal and write down everything you recall. Don't worry if it's only fragments or seemingly random details. Write down any people, places, feelings, colors, everything you can remember, no matter how small.

3. **Note the Feelings:** As you write, underline or circle the emotions you felt in the dream. Were you excited, scared, peaceful? This is just as important as the events of the dream. Sometimes a dream that looks happy (like a flying dream) could feel scary, and that emotion is a clue to its meaning. So make note of how you felt, and also how you feel as you wake up. Are you relieved? Disappointed the dream ended? Curious? All these feelings are part of the message.
4. **Reflect and Look for Patterns:** At the end of the week, read over what you've written. Do you notice anything repeating? Maybe you dreamt of different scenarios but always felt a particular emotion, or a certain person keeps popping up, or you keep finding yourself in high places or underwater. Highlight these common threads. They are your subconscious mind's favorite symbols and themes. For example, if you find you've been dreaming of flying or floating several times, consider what in your life makes you feel free or what you wish to escape from. Patterns give powerful hints about what's on your mind beneath the surface.

Keep this practice gentle and fun. Don't treat dream journaling as a chore or something you must do perfectly. Even if you only remember a tiny snippet of a dream ("something about a blue bird on a windowsill..."), jot it down. Over time, you'll likely find that you remember more and more. You're essentially telling your mind that dreams matter, and so it will serve up more details for you. Every entry in your journal is a step toward learning the unique language of *your* subconscious.

LOOKING AHEAD

My childhood flight taught me that dreams can lift us up, sometimes literally. In this chapter, we explored how even a single dream can open the door to deeper understanding: of freedom, of longing, of the unspoken parts of ourselves. We also touched on the fascinating truth that dreams aren't just poetic illusions; they're born of both subconscious insight and biological brilliance.

REM sleep, as you've now seen, is the fertile ground where most of our vivid dreams are born. During this stage, our brains are active, our emotions run high, and our subconscious begins to speak in symbols. Freud believed dreams offered a direct path into the unconscious mind, revealing repressed thoughts, hidden fears, and unresolved desires. Jung later expanded on this idea, suggesting that dreams do more than expose buried material; they also guide us toward integration and wholeness through symbols, archetypes, and inner balance. What's especially compelling is how modern neuroscience supports much of what these early thinkers sensed: that dreams are not random, but deeply meaningful reflections of both our biology and our inner life.

You've already entered this powerful inner dialogue by beginning your dream journal. Each dream you write down is more than a passing image; it's a message, a thread leading you back to parts of yourself that are ready to be seen and understood.

Some nights, your dreams may feel like puzzles or whispers from another world. Others may be clear and uplifting, like the flying dreams of childhood. No matter what form they take, they are always worth listening to. With practice, patterns emerge. Meanings unfold. A personal language begins to reveal itself.

And yet, before we can interpret a dream, we must first remember it. In the next chapter, we'll explore how to strengthen and refine your dream recall. Now that you've seen how a single dream can open doors to self-discovery, let's explore how to capture those dreams before they slip away in the morning light.

2

ENHANCING DREAM RECALL

WAKING UP WITH YOUR DREAMS

Our brains create dreams during every stage of sleep, but our ability to remember them depends on a combination of biological and behavioral factors. Neuroscience shows that waking during REM sleep, the stage associated with vivid, emotional dreaming, greatly increases the likelihood of recall. Studies reveal that 80–90% of people awakened during REM can remember their dreams, compared to less than 50% from other stages. According to the arousal-retrieval model, a brief moment of wakefulness is essential to store a dream into memory. In fact, people who frequently recall their dreams tend to wake more often throughout the night, especially during light NREM (non-rapid eye movement) stages.

NREM is the "quiet" phase of sleep, when the body slows down, breathing, heart rate, and brain activity all decrease, allowing for physical rest and repair. But dream recall is strongest when emerging from REM, where brain activity more closely mirrors waking consciousness. To preserve these fragile memories, focusing on your dream the moment you awaken is critical. Research confirms that dream content fades rapidly, often within seconds, unless we give it immediate attention. That's why sleeping long enough for rich REM cycles and waking gently (rather than with abrupt alarms or bright light) can significantly improve how much of your dream world you bring back with you.

NEUROBIOLOGY OF DREAM MEMORY

When we sleep, the brain's usual memory machines mostly shut down. Chemicals and brain signals that form long-term memories are at very low levels during dreaming. For example, the alertness chemical norepinephrine is almost gone, and activity in the front part of the brain (prefrontal cortex) is quiet. In simple terms, the brain isn't in recording mode, so if a dream finishes before you wake, it usually fades immediately. Dreams end up forgotten because their details never get stored as real memories.

- **Memory and Logic in Dreams**

Normally, the prefrontal cortex (the front of your brain that handles planning and logical thinking) helps decide what to remember. But during REM sleep, this "thinking center" turns down its activity. With the prefrontal cortex quiet, dreams often feel strange and disconnected. This lack of active "memory watchdogs" means most dreams slip away upon waking. One study even found that people who had more relaxed (theta) brain waves in the prefrontal cortex right after a REM phase were better at recalling dreams. In other words, the closer the brain is to waking (with memory circuits coming back online), the more likely a dream will stick.

- **Emotion and REM Sleep**

Deep inside the brain lie areas that stay busy during dreaming. The amygdala, an almond-shaped region that handles emotions, lights up in REM sleep. This is why dreams often carry powerful feelings. At the same time, the hippocampus (our memory hub) also shows activity in REM. This suggests dreams may weave in pieces of our recent experiences. Scientists believe REM sleep is especially good for processing emotional memories. In fact, researchers propose REM provides a "safe space" for sorting and strengthening the emotional parts of our day before we wake. In plain terms, REM dreams may help the brain replay and file away feelings, even as they happen in our sleep.

- **Waking Up and Remembering Dreams**

Timing is everything for dream recall. As the brain wakes up, memory systems switch back on. If you wake directly out of a REM dream, you catch those memory processes in action, so the dream has a good chance of being saved. But if you drift from dreaming into deep sleep without waking, you usually lose the dream permanently. That's why most dream memories come from waking right after a REM period. It also explains why vivid or scary dreams, which often jolt us awake, are the ones we tend to remember. Nightmares and very emotional dreams raise our body's alertness and wake us up, so they get recorded in memory, while more ordinary dreams disappear into the night.

WHY DREAM RECALL MATTERS ACROSS CULTURES

In many Indigenous Amazonian communities, like the Ese Eja, dreams aren't just stories but tools for survival. Recalling dreams is crucial because people use them to make decisions about hunting, fishing, and healing. If someone dreams of a certain animal or plant, it may guide what they eat, where they go, or how they treat illness. Forgetting a dream could mean missing an important message about health or danger.

For Aboriginal Australians, dream recall is deeply spiritual. "The Dreaming" is not just about sleep; it's a sacred time when ancestral beings created the land, and those stories continue to live on through dreams today. Remembering dreams is a way to stay connected to these ancestors and to follow cultural laws and responsibilities.

Dreams are part of daily life and passed down through art, ceremony, and oral tradition; recalling them keeps those teachings alive.

Dreams are gateways to deeper awareness in Eastern traditions, like Hinduism and Buddhism. Ancient texts teach us that dreams offer insight into our inner life, and Tibetan Buddhists even practice "dream yoga" to stay conscious while dreaming. The goal is to learn from the dream state, not just experience it. Forgetting a dream loses that chance for learning or awakening. Remembering dreams is essential to the spiritual path.

In the Abrahamic faiths, Judaism, Christianity, and Islam, dreams are often viewed as messages from God. Many key figures in scripture received guidance through dreams that shaped entire stories or destinies. Recalling those dreams was essential to receiving divine direction. To this day, many believers in these traditions pray for dreams that offer clarity, warnings, or answers. Forgetting the dream might mean losing the guidance it provided.

Despite these varied perspectives, one truth echoes: *dreams are only meaningful if we remember them*. Whether used for survival, spiritual connection, or divine insight, *dream recall* is the first step in honoring what the dream is trying to say.

Fun Fact: Herbal Teas That Support Dream Recall

Several herbal teas are renowned for their calming properties and ability to enhance dream vividness.

Valerian Root: Traditionally used as a mild sedative, valerian root can reduce the time to fall asleep and may promote deeper sleep stages associated with more vivid dreams.

- **Chamomile**: Known for its calming effects, chamomile tea may help reduce anxiety and promote relaxation, supporting better sleep quality and dream recall.
- **Lemon Balm**: Studies show lemon balm improves mood and induces mental calmness, enhancing sleep quality and leading to more vivid dreams.

- **Passionflower**: Often used to reduce anxiety and insomnia, passionflower flowers may help increase total sleep time and improve sleep quality, contributing to enhanced dream recall.
- **Mugwort**: People use mugwort to induce lucid dreams; they believe it enhances dream clarity and recall, although scientific studies are limited.

Combining these herbs in teas or supplements may provide synergistic effects, promoting relaxation and enhancing dream vividness and recall.

CULTIVATING DREAM RECALL

I wake up and stay perfectly still, clinging to the dream like it's a thread I don't want to break. That quiet moment before full consciousness feels sacred, where everything is both real and not, and the dream still lingers like steam on glass.

In the dream, I'm with Reggie—my dog, my companion of fourteen years. He's younger here, or at least moving like he used to, with that spark in his step that used to make me laugh. We're walking along a wooded trail, the kind lined with tall pines and thick air that smells like sap and sunlight. I'm tossing him his old, chewed-up tennis ball, and he's chasing it like it's the greatest treasure on Earth.

We reach a grassy hill that slopes down toward a shallow creek, the water glinting like glass. Reggie bounds up and over the hill, vanishing for a moment. Just as I'm about to follow, I hear this sharp clang—like metal hitting metal—echoing from somewhere beyond. Maybe roadwork, maybe a passing truck, or maybe something the dream made up entirely. I pause, waiting to hear him bark or come back.

But he doesn't.

Instead, everything shifts.

Suddenly, I'm somewhere else entirely. I'm in a long hallway made of glass walls, floor, everything, but it's not reflecting light the way it should. The sky above is dusky purple, heavy and low like a thunderstorm is waiting just outside view. There's no sound except the squeak of my shoes as I walk, and I realize I'm dragging something behind me. I look down and it's a folded-up lawn chair tied to a leash.

Reggie's leash.

I'm not even surprised. That's how dreams work: you just accept the bizarre. I keep walking, pulling this squeaky metal chair, which resists like it weighs a hundred pounds. I don't know where I'm going. I'm not even sure I'm supposed to find him anymore. I just feel this quiet urgency, like if I don't keep moving, something will disappear for good.

Then the world tips again.

I'm in my backyard. It's late, twilight, maybe, and the sky has that bruised purple haze, just before dark takes over. The grass is damp beneath my feet, and everything feels unnaturally still.

Then I hear it.

A long, high-pitched howl cuts through the silence. Not a dog. Not quite. It's too sharp, too stretched out. Coyotes, maybe, but it doesn't sound right. It's layered, like there are too many voices overlapping at once. Something in it chills me. There's no wind, no rustling trees. Just that eerie sound echoing through the air like a warning or a summons.

And then he appears.

Reggie comes limping out from behind the shed. No bark. No tail wag. Just quiet, steady steps—like each one is measured. His eyes find mine immediately, and they hold me there.

Then I see it.

His front leg is hanging—completely wrong. It's not just injured—it's empty. No bone. No muscle. Just skin and fur, swinging like a sleeve with nothing inside. A puppet limb, weightless and horrifying. There's no blood. No torn skin. It's almost worse that way—like something essential has just vanished, like the structure of him is dissolving.

My body goes still. That kind of paralyzing stillness you only feel in nightmares, where everything around you slows down but your heart hammers like it's trying to escape.

But Reggie doesn't look afraid.

He just gazes at me with those familiar, soulful eyes, the ones that watched me through heartbreaks and lazy Sunday mornings. Eyes that say, I didn't want you to see this. But now you do.

And in the dream, I can't move. I can only watch him stand there, brave and broken and unshaken.

Then I wake up.

I'm glad I didn't move when I woke up. I just stayed there, frozen in that in-between place where the dream still clings to you. I can still see it all: the walk through the woods, the strange sound of metal, that surreal moment dragging the lawn chair, and then the backyard—the howls, the stillness, and Reggie's leg. The shift in atmosphere was sharp, like a crack in reality. What started off light and familiar turned eerie and hollow. That image—his leg just hanging there, like it had lost its structure—still sits heavy in my chest. I don't know if my mind was trying to prepare me for something or just echoing fears I haven't named yet. But it didn't feel random. It felt like a message I haven't quite understood.

That morning taught me something important about dream recall: our morning routine can make or break our memory of the night's dreams. If I had leapt up to start my day, I might have lost that precious scene of Reggie forever. Psychologists even have a term for this idea. They call it the salience-interference hypothesis. In plain language, our brain tends to let dreams fade away quickly unless we grab onto the most salient (emotional or important) parts before thoughts of breakfast or to-do lists overwrite them. Emotional dreams, like one with a beloved pet, naturally feel more significant, so they're easier to remember if we pay attention to them when we wake. In other words, by remaining still and gently replaying my dream, I gave it importance in my mind. The result was that the vivid image of

Reggie stayed safe in my memory, not lost to the busy noise of the morning.

Everyday Habits for Better Recall

Over time, I've learned simple, practical habits that help me remember more dreams. You can try them too. Here are some key practices that have worked for me (and many dream researchers recommend them):

- **Sleep consistently:** Aim for 7–9 hours of sleep each night, and go to bed and wake up at about the same times. A steady schedule helps your brain cycle naturally through all sleep stages, including the longer REM periods later in the night. (REM is when the most vivid dreaming happens.) When you're well-rested and in sync, your chance of remembering dreams the next morning goes up.
- **Optimize your sleep environment:** Make your bedroom a dream-friendly zone. Keep it cool, dark, and quiet. Avoid screens, bright lights, or stressful activities right before bed. For example, I turn off my phone an hour before sleep and read a calming book. This kind of evening routine relaxes the mind and leads to deeper sleep. The more uninterrupted sleep you get, the more REM sleep you'll enjoy, and the more stories your mind can create and retain.
- **Keep a dream journal:** Always have something to write with on your bedside table. It can be a notebook or even a voice recorder. As soon as you wake (before distractions set in), jot down any images, feelings, or words from your dream. You don't need a perfect narrative, bullet points or a few key phrases help. This habit tells your mind, "This is important." Over time, your brain will start prioritizing dreams it knows you'll record, making recall easier.
- **Set an intention:** Before falling asleep, gently tell yourself, "Tonight I will remember my dreams." This simple intention can prime your subconscious to pay attention. I sometimes visualize holding onto a dream as I drift off, like saving a file

before shutting down a computer. It sounds a bit magical, but many people find that this quiet intention makes their dream images sharper in the morning.
- **Be still on waking:** This is the magic step that helped me remember Reggie's dream. When you wake up, resist the urge to jump out of bed or immediately reach for your phone. Lie still for a minute with your eyes closed. Replay your dream in your mind as if you're watching it on a screen. Feel its emotions again. This gentle focus locks the memory in. Imagine your mind is a camera trying to capture the dream; being still lets it take a clear picture before the day grabs your attention.

You may need patience to adopt these habits, but the effort is often worthwhile. I've gone from recalling almost no dreams to waking up with a scene or two fresh in my mind. And when dreams are vivid or emotionally charged, like the one with Reggie, these techniques make sure those dreams don't slip away.

EMBRACING REM SLEEP

You might wonder why sleep habits matter so much. The answer lies in how our brains dream. Most dreaming happens during REM (Rapid Eye Movement) sleep, especially the colorful, story-like dreams. REM periods get longer as the night progresses, especially in the early morning hours. That's why getting a full night of sleep is crucial: if you cut sleep short, you might miss the best dream segments. By sleeping well and avoiding alcohol or heavy meals before bed (which can interrupt REM), you give yourself a chance to cycle naturally into REM sleep multiple times.

Think of REM sleep as the stage where your subconscious shows its most meaningful images. The longer you allow those REM stages, the more material you have to remember. In practice, this means sleeping enough hours and treating bedtime as a sacred time. Gentle activities like meditation, reading, or listening to soft music can help your brain transition into the deep, REM-rich sleep we need for vivid dreams.

Looking Ahead: Dream Symbols

By now, you have built a bridge to capture your dreams as they happen. You've seen how stillness and small rituals helped you hold onto that clear image of Reggie, an image filled with love and insight. Your dreams are starting to feel less random and more like messages waiting to be understood.

In the next chapter, we will follow the trail of those messages. We'll learn how to translate dream symbols: the people, places, and events your subconscious sends you each night. Every detail you've learned to remember has a potential clue. Now that you're catching these clues, Chapter 3 will help you interpret them.

Keep practicing patience and presence. The quiet moments after waking are gifts where your dreams speak to you. As you continue to gather your nighttime stories, you're preparing to step into the rich, symbolic world of interpretation. Sweet dreams, and stay tuned for our journey into the language of dream symbols.

3

BREAKING DOWN DREAM SYMBOLS: COMMON SYMBOLS AND THEIR MEANINGS

Now that you've begun capturing your dreams, it's time to decode their language. Let's start by exploring the most common symbols in our nightly visions.

Journal Entry: Early Morning and still half in that dream world

Wow. I just woke up from one of the most intense dreams I've had in a long time. I can still feel it in my chest, like a low vibration that hasn't fully left my body. I don't know exactly what it means yet, but I know it meant something. I'm writing this now while it's still fresh, before it slips away like so many others.

In the dream, I was standing in front of this massive rocky mountain, or maybe it was a quarry. It loomed in front of me, towering and steep, all jagged edges and unforgiving gray. Giant industrial machines crawled slowly up and down its face, rumbling as they moved, their heavy metallic sounds echoing through the air. It felt like a place that had been worked over for decades, worn down by effort, yet still unbreakable.

Above it all, the sky hung low and dark, swollen with clouds that felt too close, like they were pressing down. There was this tension in the air, like the weather was holding its breath. Somewhere in the distance, I heard what might've been thunder, or maybe it was something more profound, something inside the mountain itself.

Then I noticed the houses. Small, tucked into the cliffs like nests carved from the rock. They looked out of place, fragile even, but warm. Light spilled from their windows, golden and calm. In that strange dream way, they made me feel safe. A kind of stillness, like life was going on despite the cold machinery and looming sky.

That's when I felt it, a faint tremor under my feet. So slight I almost ignored it. The machines paused, just for a beat, like they sensed something too. And then a sound, a low groan from deep inside the mountain, like it was waking up.

A train whistle pierced the silence.

Bright and cheerful, a colorful train curved around the mountain's edge, laughing passengers inside. It felt almost magical, like a dream within a dream. Their joy cut through the weight of the scene, and I remember smiling, just watching them pass. It was such a beautiful, human moment—something light in all that heaviness.

And then, without warning, the mountain cracked open.

It split with a deep roar and swallowed the train whole. Just like that. No screaming, no crashing metal. Only silence. An impossible silence, like the world had held its breath and decided not to exhale. I didn't scream. I didn't run. I just stood there, frozen, watching the dust rise and settle like ash.

And then I woke up, heart pounding, not afraid exactly, but shaken. Moved. That dream meant something. Maybe emotional. Maybe spiritual. Maybe both. I don't have the answer yet, but I feel like my subconscious was trying to show me something big beyond language.

I'm so glad I stayed still long enough to remember it. I can still see the glow of the cliffside windows. I can still hear the train whistle. I still feel that split-second tremor before everything changed.

There's something in this dream I need to understand.

Several vivid elements stand out in that dream:

- **The Mountain/Quarry:**
  - The towering mountain, worn and worked over, felt immovable yet alive, almost sentient. Mountains often symbolize life's greatest challenges, but here, the looming stone carried something more: tension, pressure, and the sense that something long buried was about to surface. It reflected not just obstacles, but a shift waiting to happen—one that couldn't be held back much longer.
- **Industrial Machines:**
  - The grinding, crawling machines suggested relentless effort. They echoed the feeling of being caught in systems that are bigger than us—daily routines, responsibilities, and emotional labor. Their mechanical noise felt oppressive, highlighting how life can sometimes keep moving without offering any space to breathe or reflect.
- **Homes Built into the Cliff:**
  - These tiny, glowing homes were the emotional contrast to the harshness around them, offering a sense of human warmth in a place of heavy machinery and looming skies. Their presence symbolized resilience, community, and the quiet safety we try to build in even the most unstable places. But their position, perched high and fragile, also whispered of vulnerability and the effort it takes to hold onto that comfort when everything around you feels like it could fall.
- **The Train:**
  - The bright, almost magical train carried laughter and life: hope, momentum, connection. It moved through the dream like a thread of joy in the dark. But its sudden disappearance felt like a deep emotional rupture, perhaps representing the fear of losing something beautiful just as you reach it, or the unpredictable nature of joy itself. It could symbolize sudden loss, or the idea that transformation often demands letting go.

- **The Sky and Tremor:**
  - The heavy clouds above were more than weather; they were emotional atmosphere. They foreshadowed change, and the subtle tremor before the mountain cracked gave a physical warning. These elements built the tension and pointed to an internal truth: something was shifting beneath the surface. The dreamer's stillness in the face of the eruption may reflect how we freeze when the unexpected happens, even when we've felt it coming all along.

Each of these powerful images left me with a sense of meaning just beyond my grasp. In the rest of this chapter, we will gently unpack more dream symbols and their meanings, piece by piece. Together, we will learn to listen to the secret language of dreams and what they are trying to tell us. The journey into their meanings begins now, and step by step, we will discover the wisdom hidden within our nightly visions.

COMMON DREAM SYMBOLS

Dream symbols often feel mysterious, but science suggests they're tied to our emotions and daily experiences. That means a symbol you see in a dream likely connects to how you feel or what's going on in your life. Importantly, experts note that there's no single "dictionary definition": the meaning of a dream image can vary by person. In the list below, we use simple language to describe some of the most common symbols. Think of these as general ideas and remember to mix them with your own story and feelings.

- **Flying:** Flying dreams usually feel uplifting. They often symbolize freedom, confidence, or a burst of motivation. (If flying was frightening or out of control, it could instead suggest stress or a wish to escape.)
- **Falling:** Nearly everyone has fallen in a dream at least once. This typically mirrors fear or anxiety in waking life. For

example, falling may point to feeling out of control, unsupported, or nervous about taking a risk.
- **Teeth (falling out):** Losing teeth in a dream is startling. People often interpret it as feeling a loss of something important (like confidence, health, or a relationship). These dreams also tend to pop up when stress is high or you feel a lack of control.
- **Water:** Water is a very common symbol, linked to emotions and the unconscious. Calm, clear water may suggest peace or emotional balance, while turbulent waves or deep water can reflect strong feelings or being overwhelmed. In general, think of water in your dream as pointing to how you really feel "below the surface".
- **Snakes:** Snakes can be scary, but they don't always mean danger. Often, a snake hints at hidden fears or life changes. For many, snakes symbolize deep-seated anxiety or a challenging situation. On the positive side, a snake shedding its skin in a dream can represent personal growth or transformation.

It's helpful to note how you felt about each symbol. For instance, flying might mean pure joy or secretly wanting to run away: context matters. Similarly, falling dreams almost always connect to anxiety or feeling unsafe. Pay attention to whether the water felt friendly or threatening, or if the snake was calm or aggressive. Your emotions and the details (bright day vs. dark storm, gentle stream vs. raging river) will tune the symbol's meaning.

- **Vehicles (cars, bikes, etc.):** Vehicles in dreams often represent your life's journey. Driving or riding a car can mirror how you feel about where you're headed. If the vehicle runs smoothly, it might mean confidence; if it's out of control or breaking down, you could feel anxious about your direction. In short, vehicles point to your sense of control and direction in waking life.
- **Houses or Rooms:** A house often stands for you or your mind. Different rooms can symbolize aspects of yourself or

memories. For example, a messy room might hint that some thoughts or feelings are chaotic, while discovering a new room could mean uncovering a hidden talent or memory. Dream experts say a house dream is like looking at the rooms of your mind.

- **Being Chased:** This is one of the most common dreams. If something is chasing you, it usually means you're avoiding an issue or feeling chased by stress in real life. The chase itself signals anxiety: you may feel pressure or fear that something bad will catch up to you. Who or what was chasing you can offer clues about what you're running from.
- **Elevator (or Escalator):** Dreaming in an elevator box taps into feelings of control. Researchers note elevator dreams often involve anxiety and a sense of helplessness. Riding up may feel hopeful or indicate progress, while going down can reflect setbacks or worries. Sudden drops or malfunctions in an elevator dream usually point to feeling unstable or shocked by events in life.
- **Death or Dying:** Seeing death in a dream isn't literal. It often symbolizes an ending or a big change. Many people wake up relieved after a dream of death, because experts say it usually means you're moving on to a new phase. It could mean something in your life needs to "die", like an old habit or situation, to make room for a fresh start.

Personal context is key for these symbols. A dream about a car speeding might stress you if your life feels rushed, but might thrill you if you love adventure. Remember, experts stress that dream meanings are personal and subjective. The same image can mean very different things to two people. Use these general ideas as a starting point, but always relate them to your own life. For example, if you love snakes (or fear them deeply), that will change what a snake symbol means to you.

- **Exam or Test:** Dreaming you're unprepared for a test (even as an adult) usually signals stress or self-doubt. It can mean you

fear being "tested" in some way, maybe at work or in a relationship. Basically, it reflects worry that you might not be ready for a challenge.
- **Being Trapped or Stuck:** If you dream your legs won't move or you're caught in a tight space, it often mirrors feelings of frustration or helplessness. You might feel in real life that something or someone is holding you back. The dream symbol means something is blocking you until that obstacle is removed.
- **Being Lost:** Finding yourself lost and unable to locate your home or escape in a dream often signifies feelings of uncertainty or a lack of confidence. It reflects a waking life filled with indecision, highlighting fears that you might not achieve your ambitions or that you're straying from your intended path.
- **Being Naked in Public:** Dreaming of public nudity feels embarrassing, and that's exactly what it usually means. It signals vulnerability and fear of exposing your flaws or secrets. You might feel insecure or worry that others will see your "weaknesses." In friendly terms, it's your mind telling you it's okay to feel exposed, but you're ready to address it.

Every dream symbol comes with layers of meaning. Psychologists remind us that dreams help process our emotions, so symbols often tie directly to things we care about. Yet no interpretation is absolute. Think of these meanings as gentle clues. Notice how you felt in the dream (scared, excited, calm) and what's happening around the symbol. As you explore your dreams with curiosity, you'll see how personal history and emotion shape each symbol's story. Enjoy this adventure into your subconscious and stay open-minded.

EXPLORING SYMBOLS ACROSS CULTURES

While many dream symbols feel universal, like flying, falling, or being chased, their meanings can shift depending on your background, beliefs, or upbringing. Dreams aren't just personal; they're also shaped by the stories, traditions, and symbols passed down through generations. In other words, what you dream might mean something entirely different to someone else on the other side of the world.

In this next section, we'll explore how different cultural traditions interpret common dream symbols such as animals, water, and light. You'll see how different cultures interpret the same image, such as a snake or an owl, as either sacred or unsettling. These brief snapshots offer a richer, more colorful lens for understanding your own dreams, one that honors the global wisdom that's shaped how humans have made sense of the dream world for centuries.

Let's examine how four cultural perspectives—Western, Indigenous, Eastern, and African/Latin American—view dream symbols.

Western Perspectives

In Western culture, old stories, religion, and psychology shape many dream symbols. For example, dreaming of an owl might make people think of wisdom, thanks to ancient myths like the Greek goddess Athena, whose symbol was an owl. A snake might feel scary, but in Western traditions, it can mean danger (like the snake in the Garden of Eden) or healing (like the snake wrapped around a doctor's staff). Water often reflects how we're feeling inside; peaceful when it's calm, overwhelming when it's stormy. Dream journeys, such as driving or walking down a long road, often signify life changes like starting a new job, moving, or personal growth. Western psychologists typically interpret these dream symbols as reflections of one's inner thoughts and emotions.

- **Owls:** In Western dreams, people usually see owls as wise and thoughtful. This comes from old stories like the Greek goddess Athena, who had an owl as her symbol. If you dream of an owl, it might mean you're searching for insight or that your inner wisdom is trying to speak up.
- **Snakes:** Snakes can be tricky in Western dreams. They might appear as something dangerous, like temptation or betrayal, but they can also represent healing and change. It depends on

the feeling of the dream. A scary snake might point to hidden fears, while a calm one might mean you're ready to grow or shed something old.
- **Water:** Water usually reflects your emotions. Calm, clear water can mean peace or emotional balance. But if the water is rough or flooding, it may suggest you're feeling overwhelmed, stressed, or dealing with something that's hard to manage.
- **Journeys (roads, cars, travel):** Dreaming of traveling, whether walking, driving, or being on a long road, often represents change or progress. It can mean you're going through a transition in life, figuring out your direction, or moving forward in some area of your personal journey.

INDIGENOUS TRADITIONS

For many Indigenous cultures, dreams aren't just random images but sacred messages. Many see dreams as bridges between the physical world and the spirit world, offering guidance from ancestors, nature, and unseen realms. They're deeply connected to community, ritual, and a respect for the land. Symbols in these dreams often carry stories passed down through generations, filled with meaning that shapes real-life decisions.

Here are some of the most powerful symbols found in Indigenous dream traditions:

- **Snakes:** Many Native traditions view snakes positively. They're not just creatures to fear, but symbols of life, healing, and renewal. Some tribes, like the Pueblo, associate snakes with fertility and the cycles of the Earth. For the Ojibwa, a snake shedding its skin in a dream can mean rebirth or deep transformation; a sign that something new is beginning.
- **Owls:** In several Indigenous cultures, owls are mysterious and powerful messengers. Their appearance in dreams often signals a connection to the spirit world. People might

- interpret an owl's night call as a warning, a sign of change, or even a visit from an ancestor. Although people respect owls, they can also inspire fear, not because owls are evil, but because they reveal truths we may not want to face.
- **Water:** Water is much more than just a symbol; it's sacred. People see dreams of rivers, rain, or lakes as messages from the natural world. In many Indigenous beliefs, water is a living spirit, a source of wisdom, cleansing, and emotional healing. If you dream of water, it may invite you to listen more deeply, wash away what no longer serves you, or reconnect with your roots.
- **The Journey (Man in the Maze):** Some tribes, like the Tohono O'odham and the Navajo, use powerful symbols like the "**Man in the Maze**" to represent life's journey. Dreaming of roads, paths, or mazes may reflect your spiritual walk, your choices, challenges, and the way you navigate life. These dreams often prompt reflection: *Are you following your true path? Are you moving with purpose?*
- **Animals (Bears, Eagles, Wolves):** Many Indigenous traditions believe that animals in dreams are spirit guides or protectors. A bear might represent strength and introspection. An eagle could signify vision, freedom, or a connection to the Creator. A wolf might symbolize loyalty to the pack or the need to walk alone for a while. These animals don't just appear; they visit you with a purpose.

In Indigenous cultures, dreaming is not something to brush off. It's part of daily life, respected as a source of wisdom, healing, and connection. Whether your dream brings you a snake, an owl, or a winding path, it may be more than just a symbol—it may be a message from your ancestors or the Earth itself.

EASTERN TRADITIONS

In many Eastern cultures, such as those in India, China, Japan, and Tibet, spirituality, energy, and the search for inner balance are deeply incorporated into dreams. People often view dream symbols not just as signs, but as reflections of the soul, karma, or one's connection to a greater cosmic order. Dreams may be messages from the divine, the self, or even glimpses of enlightenment trying to come through.

Here are a few dream symbols that carry powerful meaning across Eastern traditions:

- **Snakes:** In much of Asia, people view snakes not as threats, but as sacred beings. The snake is one of the twelve zodiac signs in China, representing wisdom, intuition, and even good fortune. In Hinduism, snakes (called Nāgas) are deeply spiritual, sometimes guarding sacred spaces, other times coiled beneath gods like Shiva. To dream of a snake here often means spiritual awakening, deep transformation, or a shedding of the past. Unlike Western fear of snakes, people here respect and revere them.
- **Owls:** While owls are wise symbols in the West, their presence in Eastern dreams can be more mysterious. Many Asian cultures consider owls omens of change or misfortune. You may interpret the owl's call as a warning of shifts or things needing your attention in your life. In some traditions, dreaming of an owl might be a sign to slow down and look more carefully at what's happening around you.
- **Water:** In Eastern dreams, water often represents purification and life force energy (like "chi" or "prana"). A dream of a calm river or pond may reflect inner clarity, emotional peace, or a spiritually "clean" space. Flowing water can also symbolize karma or the passage of time, gently reminding you to stay in harmony with life's rhythms. If the water is rough, it may signal an imbalance or emotional struggle, but still with the potential for healing and growth.
- **Journeys:** Traveling dreams, especially walking alone or climbing a mountain, often represent a spiritual path or personal evolution. In Buddhist and Hindu beliefs, these journeys might reflect movement along your dharma (life's

purpose) or spiritual learning. You might not even know where the dream path is leading, but that's part of the wisdom: the journey is the lesson. These dreams often come when you're being called to grow, reflect, or change.

- **Lotus Flowers:** While not in the original list, this symbol is worth mentioning. The lotus flower is one of the most sacred dream images in the East. Growing out of muddy water, it blooms clean and untouched. Dreaming of a lotus can mean inner strength, spiritual purity, or rising above life's challenges with grace.

Eastern dream traditions remind us that dreams aren't just mental noise; they can be quiet nudges toward harmony, insight, and awakening. If you've ever dreamed of water, a long path, or even a snake crossing your way, your inner world might be inviting you to pause, reflect, and come back into balance.

AFRICAN & LATIN AMERICAN TRADITIONS

Across Africa and Latin America, dreams are deeply spiritual. They're often seen as a form of communication with ancestors, nature, and the divine. Symbols that appear in dreams aren't just images, they're part of living traditions, shaped by powerful myths and cultural memory. In these regions, dream symbols carry stories of magic, transformation, and sacred warning.

Let's look at how some of the most meaningful symbols show up in these dream traditions:

- **Snakes:** In many Mesoamerican cultures, people honor snakes, not fear them. The Aztecs believed in Quetzalcoatl, the Feathered Serpent, a wise, god-like being who brought knowledge, learning, and even the sun itself. To dream of a snake in this tradition might point to divine insight, personal growth, or the beginning of a transformation. In some African

cultures, snakes can also represent ancestral spirits or guardians, protecting sacred knowledge.
- **Owls:** Western stories often link owls to wisdom; however, they carry a more serious meaning here. In many African and Caribbean traditions, the call of an owl is seen as a warning; a signal of death, illness, or spiritual disturbance. Dreaming of an owl in these cultures may mean you're being asked to pay close attention. It's not necessarily a bad omen but a sign that something in the unseen world is stirring.
- **Water:** Water is deeply sacred across both African and Latin American cultures. In West Africa, Mami Wata (Mother Water) is a powerful mermaid-like goddess who appears in dreams to offer fertility, healing, or transformation. In Caribbean and South American traditions, she has sisters, La Sirena, Maman d'Eau, all representing the mystical power of water. Dreaming of rivers, rain, or oceans might mean you're standing at the edge of change, or being called to reconnect with your emotions and intuition.
- **Darkness and Light:** In some traditions, nighttime isn't something to fear; it's a doorway to the ancestors. A dark cave might be a place of deep initiation. A full moon could guide you to wisdom or clarity. Many believe that dreams of darkness or moonlight are spirit-led messages that urge individuals to explore within themselves or have faith in the unseen.

These dream symbols reflect a beautiful truth in African and Latin American traditions: that dreams are alive. They're not just psychological: they're spiritual. Whether you dream of a serpent winding through the forest, a river glowing under moonlight, or a whispering owl on a branch, there may be a deeper message coming through, one filled with mystery, magic, and meaning.

As we reflect on these global perspectives, it's clear that symbols carry unique meanings shaped by our cultures, backgrounds, and personal stories. A serpent might whisper of transformation in one tradition, while in another, it slithers through tales of danger or wisdom. This rich cultural tapestry shows us how dreams speak in many voices and yet beneath these diverse interpretations lies a shared human experience, a universal language that echoes across time and place.

This is where the groundbreaking work of Sigmund Freud and Carl Jung comes in. In the next chapter, we'll explore how these two pioneers of dream interpretation uncovered the hidden layers of our unconscious minds. Freud saw dreams as windows into our deepest desires and fears, while Jung wove connections between personal symbols and the collective stories of humanity. Together, their ideas build on the cultural wisdom we've encountered, offering a psychological lens to decode the serpents, rivers, and owls that dance through our nights.

4

ADVANCED DREAM SYMBOLISM

A Memory from When I Was Eight: The Gray Figure

When I was eight, just a few days after my brother passed away, something strange happened. I was lying in bed, sharing a room with my sister, staring into the dark. The room felt heavy, like everything was too quiet. Then I saw a gray, smoky shape floating across the ceiling. It wasn't scary or mean, just kind of drifting there, like a cloud lit up by the moonlight. It didn't have a face or anything clear, just this blurry, moving form.

I gasped and yelled out loud. Right away, my sister screamed too, like she saw it in her sleep. Our mom rushed in, flipped on the light, and found me sitting up, squeezing my pillow tight, my heart racing. She hugged me close and said, "You're okay, you're safe," until I calmed down. Even then, that gray shape stuck in my head. It felt like it was trying to tell me something, but I was too young to figure it out.

By the time I was older, I began to study dreams. That is when I learned about archetypes, the universal symbols that can arise from our unconscious. Carl Jung, the famous psychologist, described archetypes as deep, inherited patterns of the psyche. He wrote that in dreams, "the most far-fetched mythological motifs and symbols can appear" spontaneously, coming from what he called our *collective unconscious*. In other words, the gray figure on my ceiling might not have been a random trick of the mind at all, but an archetypal image trying to speak through my dream.

For Jung, archetypes are the universal characters or themes that live in every human mind. They appear in fairy tales, myths, and dreams worldwide. Because these symbols are so ingrained, Jung believed that many people often dream of the same kinds of things with similar meanings. In this way, my personal experience could also be part of a larger human pattern. The gray, misty shape I saw might have represented the archetypes of grief, loss, or guidance that all people share, even in different forms.

Common archetypal figures that often appear in dreams include:

- **Shadow:** The Shadow is the dark or hidden side of the personality. In dreams, it might appear as a dark figure, a monster, or a phantom. The Shadow represents the feelings, fears, or memories we've tucked away and aren't fully aware of. (For me, that gray cloud could very well have been a Shadow-image of my sadness.)
- **Wise Old Man/Woman:** This archetype represents wisdom, guidance, or protection. It often shows up as a mentor, teacher, or loving elder in dreams, offering advice or comfort. (My mother rushing in felt caring, but that silent shape in the ceiling could have been a kind of ancestral figure or guardian spirit.)
- **Hero:** The Hero archetype symbolizes courage and overcoming challenges. Heroes in dreams often go on quests or face trials. Encountering a Hero figure can mean the dreamer is finding strength within to deal with difficulties.
- **Self:** This stands for wholeness and integration. When the Self archetype appears (sometimes as a complete figure, circle, or light), it suggests a sense of unity in the psyche.
- **Trickster:** A playful or mischievous figure. The Trickster

injects humor or chaos into a dream, breaking routines and prompting change.

Each of these archetypes carries deep meaning. My gray figure could fit into one or more of them. Perhaps it was part of the Shadow, reflecting the deep sadness and fear I felt after my brother's death. Or it might even have been a gentle guide, a voice without words, like a version of the Wise Old Man or Woman archetype, helping me navigate that scary time. Archetypal images like these give our dreams a structure and a message. They help translate our intense feelings (like grief) into symbolic scenes that the sleeping mind can process.

In fact, Jung believed our dreams work to bring unresolved issues into focus and eventually toward resolution. Modern analysts use dreams for this very reason. Dream work is often about unveiling these hidden archetypal "complexes," making them conscious so we can deal with them. For instance, therapists have found that guiding someone to explore a dream symbol can help them understand and heal emotional wounds.

This matches what grief experts have observed. Research shows that **dreams of deceased loved ones** are quite common and often healing after a loss. One study found that such dreams "occur frequently" and can be "highly meaningful," helping people come to terms with death. Many bereaved people report comforting dream visits or messages from the lost person. In this light, my dream was not just a scary fluke; it was part of how my mind was processing my brother's death. The image was strange and mystical, but it helped me subconsciously cope.

Even today, scientists are digging deeper into dreams and archetypes. One recent study used a method called motif analysis on people's dreams and noted that recurring dream themes (like dreaming of a child or a journey) may actually function as Jungian archetypes of change. In other words, the symbols that keep showing up in our dreams seem to signal important shifts in our psyche. This modern research supports Jung's old idea that dreams use these universal patterns.

Looking back, that childhood vision taught me something profound. It was intensely personal, tied to my own grief, yet it felt deeply universal, too, as if it were part of a story shared by everyone who has loved and lost. That gray, floating figure was more than a scare; it was an archetypal symbol coming through my dream.

My memory of that gray figure at eight years old opened a door to understanding archetypes, those universal symbols that speak to something deep inside us all. It showed me how a single dream image can carry meaning tied to our personal experiences and shared human stories. Now, let's dive deeper into how these dream symbols work, exploring how their meanings shift and layer depending on your emotions, life events, and unique perspective. In the next section, we'll unpack layered symbolism and contextual interpretation, revealing how to decode the rich messages your dreams are trying to share.

UNLOCKING ARCHETYPES: CARL JUNG AND PRACTICAL INTERPRETATION

Carl Jung believed that dreams were more than nighttime mental activity; they were profound symbolic expressions of the psyche. Central to his theory was the idea of archetypes: universal, inherited templates or figures residing in the collective unconscious. These archetypes appear in dreams not just to be admired or interpreted intellectually, but to be worked with, dialogued with, and integrated into personal growth.

Jung's model emphasized that dreams serve a compensatory function, balancing conscious attitudes by bringing neglected material into view. For example, someone who sees themselves as overly logical might dream of being guided by a mystical or irrational figure, representing the archetype of the Wise Woman or Mystic, inviting balance.

Applying Archetypes Practically:

Here are key archetypes and how they often appear in dream life:

- **The Shadow:** The rejected parts of ourselves—anger, fear, shame—personified in dreams as enemies, monsters, or dark strangers. To work with a Shadow figure, ask: *What trait does this figure carry that I deny in myself?* Bringing awareness to this part of you helps reduce its power.
- **The Anima/Animus:** Inner representations of the opposite gender—your inner masculine (Animus) or feminine (Anima). Dreams of a mysterious woman or assertive man may signal a call to integrate traits like nurturing or decisiveness.
- **The Self:** This archetype represents wholeness and the unification of opposites. It may appear as mandalas, radiant figures, or harmonious landscapes. When you dream of something deeply serene or unifying, the Self may be inviting you to embrace inner balance.
- **The Child:** Often symbolizes new beginnings, vulnerability, or the potential for growth. A child in a dream may reflect a neglected aspect of your potential, or a part of you needing protection and nurturing.
- **The Wise Old Man/Woman:** Teachers, elders, or guides in dreams who offer wisdom during times of confusion. If this figure appears, reflect: *What am I ready to learn that I've been resisting?*

Famous Example: Jung's House Dream

One of Carl Jung's most iconic personal dreams involved exploring a multilevel house. In this dream, he began on the top floor, a modern, well-lit space. As he descended, the rooms grew older in style and construction. He passed through medieval chambers, then reached a Roman cellar, and finally discovered a primitive, cave-like basement beneath it all.

Jung interpreted this dream as a vivid metaphor for the psyche:

- **Top floor:** Representing the conscious mind—the self we show to the world, modern and constructed.
- **Middle floors:** Reflecting the personal unconscious—our memories, repressed feelings, and past experiences.
- **Basement and cave:** Signifying the collective unconscious—a shared inheritance of archetypes, myths, and instincts common to all humanity.

This dream became a cornerstone of Jung's understanding that the psyche is layered. Dreams of houses, especially those involving exploration or descent, often symbolize a journey into deeper parts of the self. A leaky attic could represent spiritual confusion; a locked basement door may hint at hidden fears or traumas. A new wing of the house might point to an unexplored part of your personality.

Try this: Next time you dream of a house, ask yourself:

- *What room was I in?*
- *Was I going up or down?*
- *Was the space familiar or strange?*

Mapping the structure of the dream-house may give you a symbolic blueprint of your inner world.

Jung's house dream doesn't stand in isolation; it opens the door to a living principle in dreamwork: that descent often signals transformation. As we move downward in dreams, through houses, caves, or collapsing staircases, we are often being invited deeper into the layers of our unconscious. That movement mirrors psychological integration: we confront what's buried, broken, or raw so we can begin to heal it.

Let's look at a real case where this descent was not metaphorical, but felt vividly through the dreamer's recurring nightmare.

Real Case Study: Lida's Falling Staircase

Lida, a 22-year-old student struggling with intense social phobia, sought therapy after months of experiencing a recurring nightmare. In these dreams, she would be climbing a staircase—usually in a school, office, or public place—when the steps would suddenly give way beneath her. She never hit the ground; instead, she would fall endlessly, panicked, her screams lost in the silence.

Her Jungian therapist invited her to view the staircase symbolically. They explored how the stairs represented her climb toward independence and competence in adult life. The collapse reflected a subconscious fear: that she would fail, be humiliated, or be seen as incapable. The endless fall mirrored her experience of free-floating anxiety in social situations—an inner feeling of always being off-balance or on the verge of emotional collapse.

As therapy progressed, Lida began to remember early childhood experiences of emotional invalidation and pressure to perform. Her dreams started to shift. One night, instead of falling, she found herself at the bottom of the pit, gazing upward at a distant light. In later dreams, a ladder appeared. She began climbing—not quickly or without fear, but steadily.

The appearance of the ladder was a powerful archetypal shift: from chaos to structure, from helplessness to potential. In Jungian terms, this echoed a movement from the fragmented self toward the archetype of the Self—an inner integration and the slow restoration of balance. The dream became a mirror of her healing journey, showing not only where she was broken but how she was beginning to rebuild.

Lida's case is a powerful example of how recurring dreams can serve as both symptom and solution, offering not just a window into the psyche's wounds, but a symbolic path toward restoration and growth.

Her journey shows how dream analysis can uncover unconscious wounds and help us rebuild inner stability.

Reggie's Dream: When Loyalty Meets the Uncanny

Animal dreams have a way of sidestepping logic and speaking straight to the soul. They're primal, immediate, and often carry truths we're not quite ready to say out loud. In this dream, Reggie, my dog of fourteen years, wasn't just himself. He became something more: a guide, a symbol, a reflection of how love and fear can live in the same breath.

What started as a peaceful walk transformed into a series of dream-shifts: metal clanging in the distance, a surreal hallway with a lawn chair on a leash, and eerie coyote howls in the backyard. Each twist pulled me further from the comfort of memory and into something rawer—a confrontation with change, aging, and helplessness. And then came Reggie, limping forward with a leg that had lost its structure, dangling like an empty sleeve. He didn't cry out. He didn't stop. He just looked at me, steady and knowing.

This wasn't a simple memory of loss—it was a message wrapped in archetypes, dream logic, and the quiet horror of watching what you love start to unravel.

Symbol Breakdown:

Dog (Reggie):

- *Emotional:* Deep bond, loyalty, the ache of witnessing decline
- *Psychological:* Unprocessed grief, fear of aging (in him, in me)
- *Archetypal:* The Familiar as Psychopomp—guiding between worlds, between past and present, health and frailty

The Forest Walk & Play:

- *Emotional:* Joy, nostalgia, the wish for timelessness
- *Archetypal:* Eden-like beginning—the way things were before reality intervened

The Lawn Chair on a Leash:

- *Emotional:* Absurdity, disorientation
- *Psychological:* Dragging a burden, searching for connection
- *Archetypal:* Symbol of stuck memory or emotional weight—something once lively now inanimate

The Coyotes' Howl:

- *Emotional:* Instinctual dread
- *Psychological:* External threats, aging, or mortality encroaching
- *Archetypal:* Wild messengers—voices from the subconscious, calling attention to change

The Wounded Leg:

- *Emotional:* Shock, helplessness, sorrow unspoken
- *Psychological:* Anticipation of loss, the fear of witnessing suffering
- *Archetypal:* The Wounded One—embodying vulnerability and irreversible change

Reggie's dream didn't offer closure. It wasn't about comfort. It was about recognition—about seeing the slow shift from joy to sorrow and choosing not to look away. Dreams like this don't just echo the past; they warn us of what's slipping through our fingers and ask us to make peace with what we can't hold onto forever.

A Practical Framework:

When you encounter an archetype in your dream:

1. **Describe the figure.** What is it doing? What emotions does it provoke?
2. **Identify the archetype.** Does it match one of Jung's major archetypes? What aspect of life does it reflect?

3. **Reflect symbolically.** What in your waking life might this figure represent? Is it asking for integration, awareness, or healing?
4. **Dialogue with it.** In your journal, write a short conversation between you and the dream figure. This Jungian technique helps the unconscious speak more directly.

By treating your dream figures not as puzzles to decode but as parts of your own psyche speaking symbolically, you begin to form a bridge between the conscious and unconscious mind. In Jung's view, this inner dialogue is the very essence of psychological growth.

Now, as we move into the next section, we'll explore how dreams don't just pull from our own lives; they also draw from the collective stories of our cultures. Generations have passed down ancient meanings that may root your nightly symbols, not just in your memory. Let's explore how personal experience and cultural heritage shape your dreams.

THE CULTURAL LAYER: ARCHETYPES WE INHERIT

Dream symbols do more than echo our personal experiences; they also carry the weight of generations. Across every continent and era, cultures have developed unique symbolic languages rooted in myth, story, and ritual. These cultural archetypes show up in dreams just as powerfully as personal ones, offering guidance, warnings, or invitations based on collective understanding.

Take the snake, for example. In Western traditions, it often symbolizes danger or betrayal, like the serpent in the Garden of Eden. But in Indigenous North American stories, the snake is a healer, a force of renewal. In Hinduism, the coiled snake (kundalini) represents spiritual awakening. And in Chinese culture, snakes are wise, intuitive, and deeply connected to the flow of life. A dream of a snake can mean wildly different things depending on what cultural lens you're using.

Cultural archetypes aren't just fixed meanings; they're alive in our upbringing, values, and communities. Whether you've been raised in a spiritual household, a secular one, or somewhere in between, the stories you've absorbed shape the way you dream. That's why two people can dream the same symbol and wake up with entirely different gut feelings about what it means.

Here are a few other cross-cultural archetypes and how they appear in dreams:

- **The Ancestor (Guide Archetype):** In many African and Indigenous traditions, ancestors are seen as intermediaries between the human and spirit worlds. Dreams involving ancestors may feature known or unknown elders offering guidance, healing, or warnings. These figures often appear in liminal spaces—doorways, thresholds, or in twilight settings—suggesting their role as spiritual bridges. For example, a dream of an unknown elder touching your shoulder during a health crisis might be interpreted as an ancestral call toward self-care or ancestral lineage healing. These figures may appear as elders or spirits offering advice, protection, or correction. Their presence is often sacred.
- **The Trickster:** Found in Native American (e.g., Coyote), West African (e.g., Anansi the spider), and Norse (e.g., Loki) traditions, the Trickster archetype appears in dreams as a rule-breaker, shapeshifter, or comic disruptor. This figure might cause confusion, reversal, or surprise, but always with the intent to shake the dreamer out of a rigid way of seeing. For instance, dreaming of a talking animal that gives nonsensical advice might initially seem absurd, but it can provoke insight about control, spontaneity, or authenticity. (e.g., Coyote), In West African (e.g., Anansi the spider) and even Norse (e.g., Loki) traditions, the trickster archetype causes disruption but also teaches adaptability. A dream involving chaos or inversion might signal that you're being challenged to see differently.

- **The Sacred Feminine:** In many Eastern and Western traditions, this archetype appears as goddesses, healers, or protectors who embody compassion, creation, and inner power. Durga, Isis, Mary, or even archetypal mothers or wise crones can appear during times of personal crisis, fertility shifts, or deep healing. A dream of being embraced by a glowing woman in white during grief might symbolize the reawakening of emotional nurturing or divine comfort. Goddesses like Durga or Kuan Yin appear in dreams to embody strength, compassion, or fierce protection. In Western mysticism, she might emerge as the Virgin Mary, a wise crone, or a nurturing mother figure. This archetype often comes during times of emotional need or spiritual searching.
- **The Warrior/Hero:** A central archetype in many traditions, the Hero often emerges in dreams when the dreamer is confronting trials or on the verge of a breakthrough. Whether represented as a warrior, a protector, or a determined version of oneself, this figure signals resilience, purpose, and courage. A dream of wielding a sword to protect someone else might indicate the psyche is activating inner strength to set boundaries or face adversity. This archetype represents resilience and purpose. From Hercules to the samurai, dreams of facing battles or quests may call you to step into your inner strength.
- **The Dream Messenger (Shamanic Archetype):** In cultures such as Indigenous Australian, Amazonian, or Tibetan lineages, dreams are sacred portals. Dream messengers may appear as animals, natural elements, or ancestral spirits who deliver symbolic or literal guidance. A person dreaming of following a glowing bird through a forest may later interpret the dream as a shamanic calling or reminder of a forgotten spiritual path.—such as Indigenous Australian, Amazonian, or Tibetan practices—dreams are portals. Seeing birds, smoke, water, or fire may not be symbolic in the Western psychological sense, but literal journeys or messages from the spirit realm.

A Cultural Reflection Practice:

When you wake from a powerful dream:

1. **Note the central symbol**-animal, person, place, or object.
2. **Ask what it meant to you personally.**
3. **Then ask what your culture (or one you connect with) says about it.**
4. **Look for a pattern or message that resonates across both layers.**

Dreams don't just speak in your voice—they echo the voices of those who came before you. Listening through that lens helps you reclaim ancestral insight and reawaken cultural intuition you may not even know you carry.

In the next section, we'll explore how blending personal and cultural meaning allows for deeper, more nuanced interpretations of recurring dream symbols.

BLENDING THE PERSONAL AND THE CULTURAL: A DEPTH-ORIENTED APPROACH TO DREAM SYMBOLISM

Advanced dream interpretation requires more than simply cataloging symbols—it invites the dreamer into a multilayered dialogue between self, psyche, ancestry, and collective meaning. In this space, dreams are no longer static—they become transformational acts of reflection that weave memory, identity, and mythology into something living.

Personal meanings arise from your inner emotional landscape: your fears, hopes, traumas, memories. Cultural meanings are carried in the myths, stories, symbols, and religious frameworks you grew up around—or have chosen to explore. The real power of dream interpretation lies in how these two voices interact. They do not just overlap; they challenge, stretch, and deepen each other.

Take the symbol of **a river**. On the personal level, it may recall summers by the lake or grief from a flood. On the cultural level, it may stand for the boundary between life and death (Egyptian), spiritual purification (Hindu), or the wisdom path of ancestors (West African). To move beyond either/or thinking, we ask: *What is this river in me? What is it trying to carry forward or wash away?*

Here is a more robust interpretive model:

1. **Symbol Deconstruction:** Start with observation. Is the river narrow or wide? Clear or muddy? Are you upstream or downstream? Dream symbols always appear in motion—context and setting are clues to the psyche's direction.
2. **Dual-Lens Analysis:** Examine both the emotional content and the cultural resonance. For example, a snake might provoke fear (personal trauma) but signify healing in your ancestral tradition. Can the fear itself be healed through the cultural meaning?
3. **Mythic Resonance:** Identify if the symbol evokes mythic or religious stories. Are you replaying the underworld descent of Inanna or Persephone? Are you crossing the River Styx, or bathing in the Ganges? This places your dream in an ancient narrative lineage.
4. **Time Signature:** Ask when this dream occurred in your life. Are you entering a transition? Archetypes often cluster around rites of passage—birth, separation, initiation, grief, midlife, or renewal. Patterns matter more than isolated meanings.
5. **Embodied Inquiry:** Let the dream speak through your body. Meditate or journal from the perspective of the symbol: *"I am the river. I move through..."* This deepens symbolic understanding by letting the unconscious speak.
6. **Living Integration:** A dream is not truly interpreted until it is embodied. What change does it ask of you? What does it want you to grieve, embrace, release, or reclaim?

By blending personal resonance with cultural lineage, the dreamer steps into the oldest role in the world: the one who decodes the symbols of night and brings their medicine back to day.

This is advanced dreamwork—not because it's harder, but because it demands honesty, curiosity, and reverence for mystery. We find a path toward wholeness in the overlap of personal story and collective myth.

Why This Matters

Figuring out this blend of personal and cultural symbolism isn't just cool; it's a way to know yourself better. Your dreams are like a map, showing you what's going on inside and how you fit into the world. When I looked at Reggie's dream, I saw my love for him but also bigger ideas about loyalty and change that I've heard in stories or seen in life. It made me feel connected, like my dreams were part of something huge.

You can do this too. Every dream you have is a chance to learn about yourself—what you feel, what you're scared of, what you hope for. And when you add in the cultural side, you're not just looking at your own life; you're tapping into wisdom from all kinds of people and places. It's like your dreams are a bridge between you and everyone else.

A Little Challenge

Before we move on, here's something to try: think of a dream you've had recently with a powerful symbol: a tree, a house, an animal, anything. Write down what it means to *you* (like, "The tree felt like home because I used to climb one as a kid"). Then, ask someone in your family or look up what that symbol means in a culture you're part of or curious about. Maybe trees mean growth in your community or strength in another tradition. See how those meanings mix and what they tell you about your dream. Your findings might surprise you.

This way of looking at dreams, mixing what's yours with what's shared, is like opening a treasure chest. Your dreams are full of clues, and you're the one who gets to figure them out. Let's keep going and see what other secrets your dreams are holding!

BLENDING THE PERSONAL AND THE CULTURAL: A DEPTH-ORIENTED APPROACH TO DREAM SYMBOLISM

Advanced dream interpretation requires more than simply cataloging symbols—it invites the dreamer into a multilayered dialogue between self, psyche, ancestry, and collective meaning. In this space, dreams are no longer static—they become transformational acts of reflection that weave memory, identity, and mythology into something living.

Personal meanings arise from your inner emotional landscape: your fears, hopes, traumas, memories. Cultural meanings are carried in the myths, stories, symbols, and religious frameworks you grew up around—or have chosen to explore. The real power of dream interpretation lies in how these two voices interact. They do not just overlap; they challenge, stretch, and deepen each other.

Take the symbol of **a river**. On the personal level, it may recall summers by the lake or grief from a flood. On the cultural level, it may stand for the boundary between life and death (Egyptian), spiritual purification (Hindu), or the wisdom path of ancestors (West African). To move beyond either/or thinking, we ask: *What is this river in me? What is it trying to carry forward or wash away?*

Here is a more robust interpretive model:

1. **Symbol Deconstruction:** Start with observation. Is the river narrow or wide? Clear or muddy? Are you upstream or downstream? Dream symbols always appear in motion—context and setting are clues to the psyche's direction.
2. **Dual-Lens Analysis:** Examine both the emotional content and the cultural resonance. For example, a snake might provoke fear (personal trauma) but signify healing in your ancestral tradition. Can the fear itself be healed through the cultural meaning?

3. **Mythic Resonance:** Identify if the symbol evokes mythic or religious stories. Are you replaying the underworld descent of Inanna or Persephone? Are you crossing the River Styx, or bathing in the Ganges? This places your dream in an ancient narrative lineage.
4. **Time Signature:** Ask when this dream occurred in your life. Are you entering a transition? Archetypes often cluster around rites of passage—birth, separation, initiation, grief, midlife, or renewal. Patterns matter more than isolated meanings.
5. **Embodied Inquiry:** Let the dream speak through your body. Meditate or journal from the perspective of the symbol: *"I am the river. I move through..."* This deepens symbolic understanding by letting the unconscious speak.
6. **Living Integration:** A dream is not truly interpreted until it is embodied. What change does it ask of you? What does it want you to grieve, embrace, release, or reclaim?

By blending personal resonance with cultural lineage, the dreamer steps into the oldest role in the world: the one who decodes the symbols of night, and brings their medicine back to day.

This is advanced dreamwork—not because it's harder, but because it demands honesty, curiosity, and reverence for mystery. In the overlap of personal story and collective myth, we find a path toward wholeness.

LONG-TERM DREAM PATTERNS AND LIFE TRANSITIONS

Dreams often unfold over years like chapters in a mythic story—carrying emotional threads and symbolic echoes that mature as we do. These long-term patterns are not only psychologically meaningful; they are archetypal mirrors of the deepest transformations in our lives.

Jay, a 47-year-old carpenter, began documenting a recurring dream that emerged every few months over the course of a decade. In each version, he was deep underwater—sometimes in a submerged car, other times in a sunken room—but always surrounded by silence and the pressure of depth. He could breathe, but barely. His movements were slow, his vision clouded, and above him was always a blurry shaft of light he could never reach.

At first, Jay assumed these dreams symbolized stress or overwhelm. But as he started therapy and began connecting with feelings he had buried since adolescence—grief over his father's disappearance, the shame of unspoken fears—his dreams evolved. The water remained, but he began to swim. Eventually, he encountered sea creatures—first threatening, then curious. In one powerful dream, a whale approached him and let him rest against its side.

The shift was profound. The dreams had moved from silent drowning to supported descent. The ocean, once feared, had become a container. The whale—an ancient archetype of wisdom and the unconscious—had become a guide. What began as a dream of suffocation became a dream of surrender and safety. And for Jay, this marked a real-world shift in how he processed emotions: less suppression, more presence.

These long-term patterns are deeply instructive. They reveal how dreams mark life transitions not by telling us what to do, but by showing us where we are in the journey of becoming. Symbols gain depth through repetition. Their meaning matures just as we do.

When working with your own long-term dream patterns, ask:

- **What is the dominant element or atmosphere that keeps returning?**
- **Does the relationship to that element change over time—** from fear to trust, avoidance to interaction?
- **What life event or internal shift coincided with a major change in the dream?**

Dreams don't just reflect who you are—they often anticipate who you're becoming. And when they recur across thresholds in your life, they offer a sacred rhythm: a living mythology written by your own unconscious.

Track them. Trust them. They hold a map you may not yet know you're following.

Archetypal Dreamscapes: When Symbols Cross Thresholds

Some dreams don't fit into tidy categories. They don't just reflect your current emotions or recycle the past—they mark transitions, initiate growth, or whisper from the edge of the collective psyche. These dreams carry archetypal weight. They are not random flickers of imagery but turning points, invitations, and transmissions from the deeper currents of life.

The following dream vignettes explore four such experiences—each rooted in a symbolic threshold. These stories reveal how dreams can act as spiritual initiations, reflections of the unconscious self, mirrors of global transformation, or glimpses of the person we are becoming. As you read, consider which thresholds your own dreams may be inviting you to cross.

Initiation Dreams: The Threshold of Becoming

Miriam had never remembered her dreams until midlife, when she began waking in the early hours with vivid scenes that lingered. One night, she found herself walking a narrow stone path through a dense forest. The trees were ancient, their branches so thick they blocked out the stars. At the end of the path stood a glowing doorway made of shifting light. She reached for it—but her hands passed through. Each time she dreamed, she came a little closer.

Years later, after her divorce and a return to painting, Miriam dreamt of the same path. But this time, she stepped through. On the other side stood a radiant version of herself—older, unafraid, watching from a hill. The dream left her breathless. It had marked a crossing—not into fantasy, but into self-recognition. Dreams like this don't explain change. They *initiate* it.

The Silent Figure: When the Psyche Watches

Thomas had been dreaming of the same cloaked figure since childhood. Sometimes they stood on the edge of a field. Other times, in a hallway or just outside his window. The figure never moved. Never spoke. But always returned—especially during transitions: before exams, when his father died, and the night before his wedding.

As an adult, Thomas finally spoke about the figure in therapy. He didn't feel fear—only gravity, like the figure was anchoring something wordless within him. His therapist suggested it might be a representation of the *Witness archetype*—the quiet part of the self that bears witness to life's deepest moments without intervening. Thomas began journaling after each appearance, slowly piecing together how the figure had tracked his becoming. The figure didn't act. It observed. And somehow, that was enough.

Dreams of the World: When the Personal Meets the Collective

Leila, a young environmental scientist, had recurring dreams of a great city crumbling into the ocean. At first, she thought it was stress. But then came dreams of vines reclaiming the ruins, of people building homes from salvaged stone, of children dancing in ash-turned-soil. These dreams stirred something primal—hope inside collapse.

When she studied global mythology, Leila was stunned to learn that dreams of floods, collapses, and rebirth are part of humanity's oldest symbolic cycles. From Atlantis to the Hopi's emergence stories, destruction and regeneration walk hand in hand. Her dreams weren't just about *her* anxiety—they were an echo of a shared collective grief and longing for renewal. Sometimes, dreams are not mirrors of the self, but whispers from the world soul.

The Future Self: When Who You're Becoming Calls Back

Every few years, Dan dreamed of a man who looked vaguely like him —older, steadier, calm in a way Dan had never been. The man would appear in quiet places: sitting at a fire, reading in a sunlit room, standing on a cliff as waves crashed below. Dan never spoke to him, but always woke feeling strangely homesick.

During a difficult year of burnout and loss, Dan had a final version of the dream. This time, the older man turned, looked him in the eye, and simply nodded. That morning, Dan signed up for a silent retreat he'd been avoiding. The dream didn't give him answers—it gave him *direction.* Sometimes, dreams show you who you're becoming before you're ready to admit it. These are not memories in disguise—they're invitations.

Chapter Summary: Dream Symbols as Living Guides

As you've honed your skills in interpreting dream symbols and explored their cultural significance, you may have noticed certain images, emotions, or scenarios that appear repeatedly in your dreams. These recurring elements, whether it's flying, a specific animal, or a familiar place, are known as dream signs. They act as personal markers within your dream world, reflecting patterns that hold meaning for you. Recognizing these signs is a powerful step toward not just understanding your dreams but also engaging with them in a new way.

By paying attention to your dream signs, you can train your mind to spot them while dreaming, triggering the realization that you're in a dream. This awareness, called lucidity, is the foundation of lucid dreaming, a practice where you become an active participant in your dream narrative. In the next chapter, we'll explore how to use the symbolic knowledge you've gained to step into lucid dreaming, transforming your dreams into a space for conscious exploration and deeper self-discovery.

5

THE ART OF LUCID DREAMING

THE MAGIC OF LUCID DREAMING

Imagine this: You're standing on the edge of a towering cliff, the wind whipping through your hair, the vast ocean stretching endlessly below. But instead of fear, you feel exhilaration, because you know *this is a dream*. You're in control. You leap off the cliff with a single thought, not falling but soaring through the air, flying freely over the waves. This is the power of lucid dreaming: a state where you're aware you're dreaming and can shape what happens next. It's like stepping into your own movie, where you're the director, the star, and the audience all at once. Welcome to a world where your imagination is unlimited, and your subconscious is ready to share its secrets.

Lucid dreaming is more than just a cool trick; it's a gateway to exploring your mind in a way you never thought possible. When I first learned about it, I was hooked. I'd spent years puzzling over dreams like the gray figure from my childhood or Reggie's wagging tail, wondering what they meant. But lucid dreaming? That was a game-changer. It let me step into those dreams, ask questions, and even change the story. One night, I realized I was dreaming of being chased by a shadowy figure, sound familiar? Instead of running, I turned around and asked, "What do you want?" The figure dissolved, and I woke up feeling lighter, like I'd faced a fear I didn't even know I had. That's the kind of power lucid dreaming can give you.

So, what exactly is lucid dreaming? It's when you become aware that you're dreaming while still in the dream. Sometimes, you can control what happens; fly, explore new places, or talk to dream characters. Other times, you're just along for the ride, watching with a clear head. Research backs this up: studies show lucid dreaming activates parts of your brain linked to self-awareness, like the prefrontal cortex, making it a real, measurable experience. It's not just your imagination running wild; it's your mind opening a door to deeper understanding.

Why should you care? Because lucid dreaming can do more than just make your nights fun. It's a tool for personal growth, creativity, and even healing. Imagine facing a nightmare and turning it into a peaceful scene, or practicing a speech in a dream to nail it in real life. I've used lucid dreams to work through worries, like when I dreamed of being lost during a stressful job change. Once I went lucid, I could explore the dream city, find my way, and wake up feeling more in control. Stories like these aren't rare; artists have found inspiration for songs, athletes have practiced moves, and everyday folks have solved problems in their sleep. Lucid dreaming lets you tap into your subconscious, where answers and ideas are waiting.

But it's not just about practical stuff. There's a spiritual side too. In some traditions, like Tibetan Buddhism, lucid dreaming is a way to explore your inner self or even connect with something bigger. Whether you see it as a psychological adventure or a spiritual journey, lucid dreaming is a chance to know yourself better. It's like having a conversation with your deepest thoughts, with the added bonus of flying or exploring impossible worlds.

Here's the best part: anyone can learn to lucid dream. It takes practice, but it's not some mystical skill reserved for a few. If you've ever remembered a dream or felt curious about what your mind is up to at night, you're already halfway there. In this chapter, we'll walk you through how to get started, from simple tricks to keep you aware to ways to steer your dreams like a pro. We'll also dig into the science, tackle common roadblocks, and explore how lucid dreaming can change the way you see yourself and your dreams. Think of it as an invitation to become the explorer of your own dream world, with all the excitement and wonder that comes with it.

So, grab your dream journal, get ready to ask, "Am I dreaming?" and let's dive into the magic of lucid dreaming. By the end of this chapter, you'll have the tools to step into your dreams with confidence, ready to uncover the treasures your subconscious has in store. Let's make your nights as adventurous as your days!

Why Lucid Dream?

You might be thinking, "Flying in dreams sounds awesome, but what's the big deal?" Lucid dreaming isn't just about having fun; it's like a superpower for your mind. It can help you tackle fears, spark new ideas, and even grow as a person. Let's break down why lucid dreaming is worth your time, with some real ways to improve your life.

Face Your Fears

Ever wake up from a nightmare, heart pounding, wishing you could go back and change it? Lucid dreaming lets you do that. When you're aware you're dreaming, you can face that monster chasing you or turn a scary scene into something peaceful. Studies show lucid dreaming can reduce nightmare frequency, especially for people with trauma, by giving them control. It's like therapy you do in your sleep.

Boost Your Creativity

Your dreams are a playground for imagination, and lucid dreaming puts you in charge. Artists, writers, and musicians have used it to find inspiration. Research suggests lucid dreaming taps into creative brain networks, helping you think outside the box. Whether you're stuck on a project or just want to dream up a new story, lucid dreaming can unlock ideas you didn't know you had.

Solve Problems

Ever heard of someone solving a problem in their sleep? Lucid dreaming makes that easier. You can set an intention to work on something specific, like a work challenge or a personal decision. Scientists have found that dreams, especially lucid ones, can help process complex problems by connecting ideas in new ways. It's like having a brainstorming session with your subconscious.

Grow Stronger

Lucid dreaming is a chance to practice skills or build confidence. Athletes use it to visualize moves, like a skier perfecting a jump in a dream. Studies show this kind of mental rehearsal in dreams can improve real-world performance. Plus, facing fears or challenges in dreams builds emotional strength, helping you feel more in control of your life.

Explore Your Spirit

For some, lucid dreaming is more than psychological; it's spiritual. In traditions like Tibetan Buddhism, it's called dream yoga, a way to meditate in your sleep and explore your inner self. Even if you're not religious, lucid dreaming can feel like connecting to something bigger. I've had dreams where I floated in a starry sky, feeling at peace, like I was part of the universe. That sense of wonder can carry into your waking life, making you feel more grounded or inspired. It's like a little gift from your subconscious, reminding you there's more to you than meets the eye.

Why It's For You

Whether you want to conquer nightmares, get creative, solve a problem, or just have an adventure, lucid dreaming has something for everyone. It's like a gym for your mind, where you can train, play, and grow. And the best part? You're already dreaming every night; you just need to learn how to take the wheel. Let's see how you can start making that happen.

Techniques to Achieve Lucidity

Now that you're excited about lucid dreaming, let's get practical. How do you actually *do* it? Proven techniques can help you become aware of your dreams; these techniques are simpler than you might think. It's like learning to ride a bike; practice makes it easier. Here are the best ways to start, with tips to make them work for you.

Reality Testing: Build the Habit

This is about training your brain to question reality. During the day, ask yourself, "Am I dreaming?" and do a quick check. Try pushing your finger through your palm; if it goes through, you're dreaming. Or read some text, look away, and read it again; in dreams, it might change. I do this when I'm waiting for coffee or stuck in traffic. Do it 5-10 times daily, and it'll carry into your dreams. One night, I checked my phone in a dream, saw the text blur, and *bam*, I knew I was dreaming. Research shows consistent reality testing increases lucid dream chances by building awareness.

Mnemonic Induction of Lucid Dreams (MILD): Set Your Mind

Developed by Dr. Stephen LaBerge, MILD is about telling yourself you'll lucid dream. Before bed, repeat, "Tonight, I'll know I'm dreaming," like a mantra. Picture a recent dream and imagine realizing you're dreaming in it. Studies confirm MILD boosts lucidity by strengthening intention.

Tip: Combine MILD with reality testing for a double boost. Spend 5 minutes visualizing before sleep to lock it in.

Wake-Back-to-Bed (WBTB): Time It Right

This one's a game-changer. Set an alarm for 5-6 hours after you go to bed, when you're likely in REM sleep (when dreams are vivid). Wake up, stay awake for 20-30 minutes, read about lucid dreaming or jot down dream notes to stay focused. Then go back to sleep, thinking, "I'll know I'm dreaming."

Tip: Adjust the awake time (15-40 minutes) to see what works best. Too tired? Shorten it; too awake? Lengthen it.

Wake-Initiated Lucid Dreams (WILD): Dive In Deep

WILD is trickier but powerful. As you fall asleep, stay aware, letting your body relax while your mind stays alert. You might see hypnagogic images—flashes of colors or shapes. Stay calm, and you can slip into a dream lucidly.

Tip: Start with MILD or WBTB until you're comfortable, then try WILD during a nap for easier transitions.

Dream Journals: Know Your Dreams

Writing down your dreams every morning is like giving your brain a map. Note every detail, symbols, feelings, and places. Over time, you'll spot patterns, like dreaming of water when stressed or flying when happy. These "dream signs" help you recognize you're dreaming. My journal showed I often dreamed of forests, and one night, seeing those trees, tipped me off to go lucid. Research backs this: journaling improves dream recall and lucidity.

Getting Started

Pick one or two techniques to try first; reality testing and journaling are great for beginners. Stick with them for a couple of weeks and don't worry if it doesn't click right away. Lucid dreaming is a skill, and like any skill, it gets better with practice. You're training your brain to wake up inside your dreams, and that's pretty amazing!

Maintaining Control in Lucid Dreams

So, you've gone lucid, congrats! You're in a dream, aware and ready to explore. But then what? Sometimes, the excitement wakes you up, or the dream slips away. This section is about staying in the dream and making it your own, from keeping things stable to steering the story.

STAYING IN THE DREAM

When you first realize you're dreaming, it's easy to get so excited that you wake up. I did that a lot at first, poof, back to my bedroom. To stay lucid, try these:

- **Spinning**: Spin your dream body like a top. It creates a physical feeling that anchors you. I spun in a lucid dream and stayed in a glowing meadow longer.
- **Hand Rubbing**: Rub your hands together to feel the texture. It keeps you grounded. I used this in a dream city to stay focused.
- **Sensory Engagement**: Touch objects, listen to sounds, or look closely at details. In one dream, I felt the bark of a tree, and it made everything sharper.
- Research shows these actions boost sensory feedback, stabilizing the dream.
- *Tip*: If the dream starts fading, shout, "Stay clear!" to refocus your mind.

Managing Excitement

That "I'm dreaming!" rush can jolt you awake. To calm down, take slow, deep breaths in the dream or focus on a boring task, like counting steps. Studies suggest emotional regulation in dreams mirrors waking life, so practice calming techniques daily.

Tip: Practice mindfulness during the day to make dream calming easier.

Taking Control

Once you're stable, you can shape the dream. Want to fly? Imagine lifting off. Want a new scene? Picture it and turn around to see it appear. You can talk to dream characters; ask them questions or guide the story. Research shows dream control improves with practice, as your brain learns to manipulate imagery.

Tip: Start small, like changing one object, before trying big shifts like new worlds.

Using Control for Growth

Control isn't just for fun; it's a path to growth. Face a nightmare figure to conquer fear, like I did with my shadowy chaser. Or use the dream to solve problems, imagine a whiteboard and brainstorm. I once "designed" a work project in a lucid dream, and it sparked real ideas. Lucid dreams can also be a spiritual practice, like meditating in a dream temple. These moments build confidence and insight that carry into your waking life.

Tip: Set a goal before sleep, like "I'll face my fear," to guide your lucid dream.

Overcoming Challenges

Lucid dreaming sounds amazing, but it's not always smooth sailing. You might wake up too soon, forget to check reality, or just not get lucid at all. That's normal! Here's how to tackle common roadblocks and keep going.

Overexcitement

The thrill of going lucid can wake you up. If your heart's racing, take deep breaths in the dream or focus on something simple, like touching a wall. Daily meditation helps, too, it trains you to stay chill (Journal of Mindfulness).

Fix: Practice calming techniques during the day and use them in dreams.

Forgetting Reality Checks

Life gets busy, and you might skip checks. Set phone reminders three times a day (e.g., morning, noon, bedtime). I forgot checks until I made them part of my routine, like brushing my teeth. Consistency is key; studies show regular checks boost lucidity.

Fix: Use a habit tracker or app to stay on top of checks.

WBTB Sleepiness

Waking up for WBTB can leave you too tired or too awake. Adjust the timing, try 15 minutes awake if you're groggy or 40 if you're wired. I found 25 minutes worked best for me. Research suggests flexible timing improves success (Sleep).

Fix: Experiment with awake time and activities, like reading vs. writing.

Inconsistent Success

Lucid dreaming isn't an everyday occurrence. There may be weeks when it seems as though your efforts are in vain, followed by periods where you experience them consecutively. It's important to recognize this as a skill that requires consistent practice through reality checks, maintaining a dream journal, and employing techniques like MILD. Research supports the value of persistence, indicating that most individuals see improvements over several months. To maintain motivation, it's beneficial to acknowledge and celebrate even the minor milestones, such as more vivid dreams or an enhanced ability to recall them.

Feeling Overwhelmed

Trying to control everything can be too much. Start small; focus on staying lucid before changing the dream. Research suggests gradual control builds confidence.

Fix: Set one goal per dream, like "I'll look around," and build from there.

Keep at It

Every challenge is a step toward mastery. Be patient, have fun, and don't stress about "failing." Lucid dreaming is about exploring, not perfection. You're learning to dance with your subconscious, and that takes time.

Advanced Lucid Dreaming

Upon mastering the basics of lucid dreaming, you're ready to explore even more profound aspects of your dream world. Think of it as advancing to the next level in an intriguing game; each step offering unique, optional challenges that further enhance your journey of self-discovery and exploration within your dreams.

Targeted Lucid Dreaming

Set specific goals for your dreams, like practicing a skill or seeking insight. Before bed, visualize your goal, like "I'll practice my guitar solo." Athletes and musicians use this to improve performance.

Dream Yoga (See Appendix A)

In Tibetan Buddhism, dream yoga uses lucid dreaming for spiritual growth. You might meditate in a dream or explore your inner self. It's like lucid dreaming with a spiritual twist, aiming for wisdom.

Shared Dreaming

This is experimental; some believe you can connect with others in dreams. There's no solid proof, but it's fun to try. In one lucid dream, I imagined meeting a friend, and we "talked"; it felt real, even if it was just my mind. Explore it with an open mind, but don't expect science to back it yet.

Exploring Subconscious Symbols

Use lucidity to dive into recurring symbols, like water or doors from Chapter 4. Ask them, "What are you?" or interact with them. This can reveal deep insights about your life.

Pro Tip: Focus on one symbol per dream to keep it clear.

Go Slow

Advanced techniques need practice, so don't rush. Start with basic lucidity, then experiment. These ideas add depth, making lucid dreaming a lifelong adventure.

The Science Behind Lucid Dreaming

Wondering how lucid dreaming actually works? It's not magic; it's your brain doing something incredible. Let's peek at the science to see why it feels so real and what it can do for you.

During lucid dreams, your prefrontal cortex. the part that handles self-awareness and decision-making, lights up, unlike in regular dreams. EEG studies show this, with lucid dreamers signaling awareness by moving their eyes in specific patterns. It's like your brain wakes up inside the dream, letting you think clearly. That's why you can decide to fly or talk to a dream character.

Lucid dreams tap into the same brain areas as waking life, like those for vision and emotion. That's why flying feels thrilling or a dream hug feels warm. Research shows REM sleep, when most dreams happen, mimics waking brain activity (*Sleep*). Your brain is basically running a virtual reality simulator.

Lucid dreaming can help with mental health. Studies show it reduces nightmares in PTSD patients by letting them rewrite the story. It's also being explored for anxiety and depression, as it builds emotional control. I found lucid dreaming eased my stress by letting me face dream worries head-on.

For most people, lucid dreaming is safe, with no major risks. Some worry about sleep disruption from WBTB, but studies suggest it's minimal if you balance it with good sleep habits. Rarely, vivid dreams might feel intense, so ease in if you're prone to anxiety. Always prioritize rest.

Science shows lucid dreaming is a real, trainable skill that blends creativity, awareness, and emotion. It's like a lab where you experiment with your mind, backed by decades of research from pioneers like Stephen LaBerge. Knowing the science makes it even cooler; you're not just dreaming; you're hacking your brain!

Interactive Exercises

Ready to jump in? These exercises will help you build lucid dreaming skills step by step. They're fun, practical, and tied to the techniques we've covered. Grab your dream journal and let's get started!

1. Dream Recall Challenge (1 Week)

For seven days, write down every dream you remember as soon as you wake up. Note symbols, feelings, and details, even if it's just a snippet. This boosts recall, making lucidity easier. I did this and went from remembering one dream a week to three or four.

Goal: Spot dream signs (e.g., flying, water) to recognize dreams later.

2. Reality Check Routine (Daily)

Do three reality checks daily for two weeks—morning, midday, bedtime. Try pushing your finger through your palm or reading text twice. Ask, "Am I dreaming?" each time. I set phone reminders and got lucid after a week.

Goal: Build the habit so it happens in dreams.

3. MILD Practice (Nightly)

Before bed, spend about 5 minutes repeating a simple phrase like, *"Tonight, I'll know I'm dreaming."* As you do this, call up a recent dream you've written in your dream journal. Pick one that had vivid imagery or a moment where something unusual happened. Replay that dream in your mind and imagine what it would've felt like to realize, *"Wait, this is a dream."* See yourself becoming lucid in that exact moment.

Goal: Train your brain to recognize dream signs and unusual details as clues you're dreaming. The more you rehearse lucidity in waking life, the more likely it is to carry into your dreams.

4. WBTB Experiment (1-2 Times a Week)

Set an alarm for 5 hours after bedtime. Wake up, stay awake 20-30 minutes (read about lucid dreaming or journal), then go back to sleep, thinking, "I'll know I'm dreaming." Try this twice a week for a month. I got my first lucid dream this way.

Goal: Increase REM sleep lucidity.

Make It Fun

Treat these like a game, not a chore. Celebrate small wins, like remembering more dreams or catching a dream sign. Share your progress with a friend; it's more fun together! These exercises are your ticket to lucid dreaming, so dive in and see what happens.

Is Lucid Dreaming Safe?

Yes, for most people. Studies show no major risks, though WBTB might disrupt sleep if overdone (Sleep Research). Balance it with good sleep habits. If you have anxiety or sleep issues, start slow and check with a doctor if you're unsure.

Can Anyone Do It?

Pretty much! Research suggests most people can learn with practice, though it's easier for some (Journal of Sleep Research). If you dream, you can aim for lucidity. Kids, adults, and beginners; all can try.

How Long Until My First Lucid Dream?

It varies. Some get lucid in days, others take months. I had my first after two weeks of reality checks and WBTB. Consistency matters, stick with the techniques, and it'll come.

Why Do I Wake Up Right Away?

Excitement often wakes you. Try spinning, rubbing hands, or deep breathing to stay in the dream. Practice calming techniques daily to make it easier (Journal of Mindfulness).

Will It Mess Up My Sleep?

WBTB can tire you if overused, but most find it manageable with practice. Studies show minimal impact if you prioritize rest (Sleep). Limit WBTB to 1-2 times a week to start.

What If I'm Scared to Control My Dreams?

That's okay! You don't have to control everything. Start by just observing lucidly. I was nervous at first but got comfy by exploring slowly. Set small goals, like looking at dream scenery, to build confidence.

Your Journey into Lucid Dreaming

Equipped with the tools and understanding for lucid dreaming, you're on the brink of exploring a new realm. Imagine flying across landscapes or conversing with dream figures like Reggie to uncover deeper insights. Initiating this journey can begin with simple steps: perform reality checks, document your dreams, or experiment with wake-back-to-bed (WBTB) techniques. Embrace each progression, from dream recall to achieving lucidity, as a victory. Lucid dreaming transcends mere novelty; it's a pathway to personal growth, confronting inner fears, sparking creativity, and connecting with the profound.

As you refine your practice, keep a journal and regularly question your reality to blend the adventurous spirit of your days with the explorative potential of your nights. Yet, when dreams persistently recur, like wandering endless hallways, trying door after door only to find yourself back where you started, take note. These aren't just loops your mind runs for no reason. They're signals, symbols with weight. Your subconscious is knocking, asking you to pay attention.

The upcoming chapter will guide you through decoding these repeating dream patterns and using lucid dreaming to step beyond the cycle. Whether it's a maze with no clear exit or a familiar setting that shifts just out of reach, we'll explore how to turn those confusing moments into powerful breakthroughs, paving the way toward deeper self-awareness and lasting transformation.

6

INTERPRETING RECURRING DREAMS

UNDERSTANDING RECURRING DREAM PATTERNS

Dreams have a way of sticking with you, especially when they keep coming back. Recurring dreams are like a song stuck in your head; sometimes haunting, sometimes puzzling, but always trying to tell you something. They loop over nights, months, or even decades, carrying messages from your subconscious about fears, transitions, or unresolved emotions.

There's one dream that's been chasing me for years. It's always the same.

Picture this: I'm trapped in a vast maze: its gray walls towering and cold, like concrete soaked with rain. The air feels tight. I walk the endless corridors with that quiet kind of panic, the kind that builds in your chest but never explodes. I don't know what I'm running from, but I know I have to get out.

Every path twists and deceives. Some lead to locked doors; others just end in dead walls. Stairwells spiral upward, but always stop short, disappearing into nothing. Elevators hum, but when the doors open, I'm right back where I started, facing that same flickering hallway light, the same feeling of going nowhere. It's a dream that always ends the same way: I'm trapped, desperate, breath quickening, never making it out. I wake up with clenched fists and a tight chest. It's like my mind is stuck in a loop; it doesn't know how to solve.

But there's another dream. One that began the same way but shifted over time.

It used to start with the same endless maze. The same doors, the same suffocating turns. But then, one night, something changed. I found a path I didn't recognize. A hallway I'd never noticed before. My fingers brushed the handle of an exit door, and instead of vanishing like always, it held firm. I turned it. The door creaked open. Light poured in. I didn't see what was beyond, just a sense of open space, something wide and waiting. But then my feet froze. I couldn't move. I stood at the threshold of escape, trembling with a mix of relief and fear, staring at a freedom I couldn't step into. I woke up, heart pounding, as if I'd almost made it.

Months later, the dream returned, but I was back at the beginning again. Same maze. Same walls. No sign of the new path. It was like starting over. The part of me that found the door remembered, but the dream didn't.

What's strange is that, in my waking life, everything was finally falling into place. My health was strong. My job felt stable and fulfilling. My kids were thriving. I was on solid ground, with a steady rhythm to my days and a sense of peace I hadn't known in years. And for a while, the maze dream vanished. It was as if the part of me that had always felt trapped had finally been heard and set free. I'd stepped through that door emotionally, even if I hadn't fully done so in the dream. It felt like real movement. Real progress.

But healing isn't always linear. And dreams have a way of circling back, checking in. So when the maze returned, I wasn't entirely surprised. A little shaken, yes, but not broken. Maybe it was just a reminder. Maybe it was my mind's way of asking: *Are you still free? Or is some part of you getting stuck again?*

That's the strange thing about recurring dreams. Sometimes they trap you in patterns that echo your waking life. Other times, they tease you with change, an unlocked door, a glimpse of escape, only to reset, as if asking: *Are you ready yet?*

This dream, repeating for years, feels like a puzzle my mind won't let me solve. Recurring dreams like mine are common; research shows that up to 75% of adults experience them at some point. They're not random; they're your brain's way of highlighting something you haven't fully faced, like stress, fear, or a past wound. For me, the maze might symbolize a life challenge, like feeling stuck in a job or relationship, while freezing at the exit could reflect my fear of change or success. By understanding these dreams, we can unlock insights into our inner world, turning restless nights into opportunities for growth.

RECOGNIZING THE PATTERNS

Recurring dreams are like echoes of your subconscious, repeating to get your attention. They often carry core themes: being lost, chased, falling, or trapped. These themes point to emotional patterns or unresolved issues in your waking life. For example, my maze dream screams "trapped," hinting at times I've felt stuck, maybe in a tough decision or a situation I can't escape. The moment I freeze at the exit feels like my mind saying, "You're so close to solving this, but something's holding you back."

Scientists suggest that stress or life transitions, such as starting a new job or navigating a breakup, often cause recurring dreams. They can also stem from deeper roots, like childhood fears or past traumas, resurfacing in vivid, repeating images. In my case, the maze often appears after stressful weeks, suggesting it's linked to feeling overwhelmed. The frozen moment might reflect a fear of moving forward, a common theme about hesitation or self-doubt in dreams.

Symbols in these dreams are key to decoding their meaning. Mazes might represent complex problems, locked doors could symbolize barriers or opportunities, and freezing might point to fear of the unknown. Colors and emotions add layers: my maze's cold, gray walls amplify feelings of isolation, while the panic mirrors real-life stress. To spot these patterns, continue writing in your dream journal. Write down every detail: the setting, symbols, and how you felt. Note the dates and frequency. Over time, you'll see connections, like how my maze dream flares up during tough times at work. This practice turns vague images into obvious messages, helping you understand what your mind is trying to say.

Transforming Recurring Nightmares

When recurring dreams turn into nightmares, they can feel like unwelcome guests, stealing your peace. These intense dreams often act as alarms, signaling unresolved fears or traumas. My maze dream sometimes tips into a nightmare, the panic peaking as I realize I'm trapped. But nightmares aren't just here to scare you; they're trying to help you face something. The good news? You can work with them to make them less frightening.

Here are some tools that have helped me and others:

- **Dream Rehearsal**: Try imagining a new ending to your nightmare before bed. One woman shared a dream where she was constantly being chased through an abandoned hotel, never able to escape. In her rehearsal, she began picturing herself turning around to face the pursuer, only to discover it was a frightened version of herself. Just this shift, adding a new choice, helped reduce the frequency of the dream. Dream rehearsal can gently rewire your subconscious, showing your mind there are other paths to resolution.
- **Visualization**: This technique involves visualizing yourself staying calm and empowered inside the dream. A man once described falling endlessly through darkness in his nightmares. In waking life, he began practicing a visualization where he slowed the fall, then imagined landing on a soft, glowing surface. Over time, his dream changed. The fear faded. Visualization works because the brain responds to

imagined experiences almost like real ones—it rehearses safety.
- **Re-entry Work**: Don't immediately distract yourself if you wake from a nightmare. Instead, try revisiting the dream with your eyes closed and change the ending while still in a semi-sleep state. One person I worked with often dreamed of losing her voice while trying to call for help. After waking, she would close her eyes and imagine speaking clearly, being heard. She said the dreams became less paralyzing and more about reclaiming power. Re-entry gives you a second chance to finish the story.
- **Create Safety**: Building a soothing bedtime ritual can help reduce stress-based dreams. Try lighting a candle, playing soft music, or doing breathwork to signal to your body that it's safe. A father who had recurring dreams of drowning began journaling three things that made him feel supported before bed. Within a month, the drowning dreams lessened. Nightmares often arise when the nervous system is unsettled—rituals create predictability and calm.

These techniques empower you to take control of your dreamscape. By practicing them, you can transform nightmares into opportunities for healing, turning fear into resilience.

When to Seek Help

Sometimes, recurring nightmares dig in so deeply they start to affect more than just your sleep. If you find yourself dreading bedtime, waking up already exhausted, or carrying a low-grade anxiety through the day, it might be time to reach out for help. Our dreams are powerful, and when they loop on fear or helplessness, they can begin to feel like prisons.

I know this firsthand. My maze dream, with its endless gray walls, locked doors, and frozen exits, has sometimes left me emotionally wrecked by morning. Even when everything in my waking life is stable, I can still wake up with that tight chest and unsettled heart. Sometimes, self-help tools work. Other times, they're not enough.

I once read about a woman who experienced a recurring dream of being trapped underwater. In the dream, she could see people standing on a dock just a few feet away, but she couldn't scream for help: her voice was always silent. The nightmare would end with her sinking. Night after night, it returned, until she began avoiding sleep altogether. Her anxiety spiked. Her body was constantly tense. She finally sought help from a trauma-informed therapist.

Through Imagery Rehearsal Therapy (IRT), she began rewriting the dream. In her imagined version, she swam to the surface. She screamed, and this time, someone turned around. That change, small as it was, began loosening the nightmare's grip. Her therapist also helped her identify the deeper fears woven into the dream: being unseen, powerless, unheard. Over time, she began to rest again, not just physically, but emotionally.

Therapies like IRT and Cognitive Behavioral Therapy (CBT) can be incredibly effective for nightmares. They help you gently reshape the stories your subconscious is repeating and shift the beliefs underneath them. If trauma is involved, a skilled therapist can help you process it safely, so your dreams no longer need to carry that weight alone.

Seeking help isn't a failure; it's an act of courage. It says: *I want peace. I deserve peace.* Your dreams are trying to say something, but that doesn't mean they get to run your life. A professional can help you listen differently, and maybe, finally, walk out of the places you've felt stuck in for far too long.

Real-Life Stories

Recurring dreams aren't just personal; they're universal, reflecting shared human struggles. Here are three stories showing how these dreams reveal profound truths and spark transformation:

- **A Soldier's War Dream**
    - Michael, a veteran, dreamed of a war-zone night after night. He was back in combat, explosions ringing in his ears, running through smoke to save his squad. Each time, he'd wake up sweating, heart pounding, unable to shake the fear. The dream mirrored his unresolved trauma from service, a weight he carried silently. Through therapy, Michael learned his dreams were his mind's way of processing guilt and loss. Using imagery rehearsal therapy, he began imagining a peaceful ending, his squad safe, and the war zone fading. He also joined a veterans' support group, finding a connection that eased his isolation. Over time, the war dreams softened, replaced by moments of calm. Michael's story shows how recurring nightmares can point to trauma, guiding us toward healing with the right support.
- **Chased Through the Shadows**
    - Lena, a young professional, dreamed of being chased through a dark forest, an unseen figure always at her heels. The fear was suffocating, and she'd wake gasping, her heart racing. The dream echoed her real-life stress: a demanding job where she felt pursued by deadlines and expectations. Reflecting on the dream, Lena realized it was urging her to confront her anxiety.12 She started journaling, noting how the chase intensified during high-pressure weeks. Using visualization, she imagined facing her pursuer, turning the dream into a moment of empowerment. Lena also set boundaries at work, reclaiming her time. Slowly, the chase dreams faded, replaced by dreams of open paths. Her story

highlights how recurring dreams can mirror daily pressures, pushing us to take control.

- **A Child's Recurring Fear**
  - Eight-year-old Sophie dreamed of a shadowy figure standing at her bedroom door, silent and unmoving. She'd wake up crying, terrified to sleep again. Her parents noticed the dream came after moving to a new city, leaving her friends behind. The figure seemed to symbolize her fear of loneliness, a child's way of processing change. With her parents' help, Sophie drew the figure, turning it into a friendly character in her stories. They also practiced bedtime rituals, like reading together, to make her feel safe.13 Over time, the figure appeared less often, and Sophie's dreams became lighter. Her experience shows how children's recurring dreams, common in 90% of cases as nightmares,14 reflect big emotions, and simple, supportive steps can transform them.

Taking Action

Recurring dreams, like my maze with its unreachable exit, are more than puzzles: they're guides. They point to fears, hopes, or challenges, urging you to pay attention. By decoding their patterns, transforming their intensity, and learning from others' stories, you can turn these dreams into stepping stones for growth. The next chapter will explore how dreams, including these persistent loops, can solve problems in your waking life, offering insights you never expected.

In reflecting on these stories, we see how recurring nightmares are potent tools for introspection and growth. They offer insights into our fears and desires, urging us to address unresolved issues in our waking lives. As we conclude this chapter, remember that these dreams are not merely tales of terror but opportunities for transformation. The next chapter will explore how dreams can guide us toward personal growth and emotional healing.

7

DREAMS THAT THINK FOR YOU – HOW THE SLEEPING MIND SOLVES WAKING PROBLEMS

THE SUBCONSCIOUS WORKSHOP: HOW DREAMS SOLVE PROBLEMS

The insights presented in this chapter draw upon a rich mosaic of scientific research, historical accounts, and anecdotal evidence, thoughtfully synthesized from the works of scholars, scientists, and storytellers who have illuminated the profound capabilities of the dreaming mind. I carefully curated these ideas from documented sources to highlight sleep's extraordinary potential for resolving waking challenges and inspiring innovation.

When you surrender to sleep, it may appear your mind retreats into silence, but nothing could be further from the truth. Far from shutting down, your brain transforms into a vibrant workshop, tirelessly processing, organizing, and innovating. This is evident during REM (Rapid Eye Movement) sleep, the stage where vivid, narrative-driven dreams unfold. In this dynamic period, your brain engages in a symphony of tasks: sorting the day's experiences, consolidating memories, processing emotions, and, remarkably, tackling problems that eluded your waking consciousness.

Have you ever gone to bed wrestling with a decision, a creative block, or an unresolved dilemma, only to awaken with newfound clarity or a spark of inspiration? This phenomenon, often called "sleeping on it," is no mere quirk of fate. During sleep, your brain activates the *default mode network (DMN)*, a constellation of regions that hums with activity when you're not focused on external tasks. The DMN fosters creative, nonlinear thinking, weaving together memories, emotions, and ideas in ways that bypass the constraints of logic. Unlike the focused, analytical mindset of your waking hours, this subconscious process thrives in freedom, forging unexpected connections and uncovering novel solutions.

This "night shift" of the mind is a cognitive superpower, one that has fueled breakthroughs across history. The brain's prefrontal cortex, responsible for logic and self-control, takes a backseat during REM sleep, allowing emotional and associative regions like the amygdala and hippocampus to take center stage. The hippocampus replays the day's events, strengthening neural connections to form long-term memories, while the amygdala processes emotional experiences, helping you navigate complex feelings. Together, these regions create a mental playground where ideas collide in unpredictable ways, often leading to "eureka" moments upon waking. Studies, such as a 2004 *Nature* experiment, demonstrate that sleep enhances problem-solving by restructuring knowledge, with participants who slept after learning a task outperforming those who stayed awake.

The quality of sleep is paramount. Deep, uninterrupted REM cycles, which occur later in a full night's rest, are essential for maximizing these cognitive benefits. Chronic sleep deprivation or fragmented rest can disrupt this process, dimming the mind's ability to generate insights. Thus, the adage to "sleep on it" is not just wisdom; it's a scientifically grounded strategy for unlocking clarity and creativity.

HISTORICAL BREAKTHROUGHS BORN IN DREAMS

The power of dreams to solve problems is not a modern revelation; it has shaped human progress for centuries. Below are vivid examples of how dreams have sparked transformative achievements, each a testament to the subconscious mind's genius:

- **Elias Howe and the Sewing Machine (1845)**: Elias Howe, an American inventor, faced a seemingly insurmountable challenge in designing a functional sewing machine. The critical issue was the needle's mechanism, traditional hand-sewing needles, with holes at the base, proved ineffective. Exhausted and frustrated, Howe dreamt one night of being captured by cannibals wielding spears with peculiar holes near their tips. Upon waking, the image lingered, sparking an epiphany: placing a hole near the needle's tip would allow the thread to form a lockstitch, the key to a working machine. This dream-inspired insight led to the modern sewing machine, revolutionizing textile production and cementing Howe's legacy as a pioneer of industrial innovation.
- **August Kekulé and the Benzene Ring (1865)**: German chemist August Kekulé grappled with the enigmatic structure of benzene, a molecule whose properties defied the linear models of his time. One night, as he dozed by a fire, he dreamt of a snake seizing its own tail, forming a circular ouroboros; an ancient symbol of unity and cycles. This vivid imagery crystallized into a groundbreaking hypothesis: benzene's carbon atoms formed a closed ring. Kekulé's dream not only solved a central puzzle in organic chemistry but also laid the foundation for countless advancements, from pharmaceuticals to materials science, demonstrating the profound impact of subconscious insight.
- **Mary Shelley and *Frankenstein* (1816)**: In the summer of 1816, Mary Shelley, then just 18, joined a literary challenge with Lord Byron and Percy Shelley to craft a ghost story. Struggling to find inspiration, she experienced a "waking dream" during a stormy night in Geneva, envisioning a scientist animating a creature with electricity, only to recoil in horror at its awakening. This haunting vision became the seed for *Frankenstein; or, The Modern Prometheus*, a novel that wove

together science, ethics, and human ambition. Shelley's dream not only birthed a literary classic but also pioneered the science fiction genre, proving dreams' power to shape cultural narratives.

- **Otto Loewi, an** Austrian physiologist, explored the mystery of nerve impulse transmission, electrical or chemical, in 1920. On the night before Easter Sunday, Loewi dreamt of an experiment involving two frog hearts, one stimulated electrically, the other not, to test for a chemical substance. Waking abruptly, he scribbled the idea, and though he couldn't decipher his notes the next morning, the dream recurred the following night. Loewi conducted the experiment, confirming that nerves release chemicals to communicate, a discovery that earned him a Nobel Prize in 1936 and transformed neuroscience.
- **Stephen King and *Misery* (1987)**: Renowned horror author Stephen King has long credited dreams as a wellspring for his chilling tales. While on a transatlantic flight, King dreamt of a fanatical reader holding a writer captive, tormenting him in a twisted act of devotion. Jotting the idea on a cocktail napkin, he developed *Misery*, a gripping novel about a novelist imprisoned by his obsessive fan, Annie Wilkes. The dream's vivid imagery fueled a story that explored creativity, fandom, and psychological terror, showcasing how dreams can inspire narratives that resonate deeply with audiences.

These narratives highlight the extraordinary capacity of dreams to access a wellspring of creativity, providing insights that go beyond our waking thoughts. Rather than being outliers, they showcase a widespread phenomenon where the mind, during sleep, transforms into a forge of creativity.

DECODING DREAMS FOR REAL-LIFE SOLUTIONS

Ever woken up from a dream with a sudden "aha!" moment, like the answer to a problem just clicked into place? That's not just a happy accident; your brain is working overtime while you sleep, coming up with creative solutions you might miss during the day. Dreams are like a secret superpower, a place where your mind can roam free without the usual distractions of work, stress, or to-do lists. When you're dreaming, your brain mixes memories, emotions, and ideas in surprising ways, often coming up with answers to challenges that feel impossible when you're awake.

Think of your dreams as a playground for your mind. While you're snoozing, your brain is busy exploring new angles, testing out ideas, and making connections you wouldn't think of during the day. It's like your subconscious is a clever friend who's always brainstorming in the background, helping you solve problems without you even trying. Scientists say this happens a lot during REM sleep, that part of the night when your dreams are most vivid and wild. It's like your brain is throwing a creative party, and the guest list includes all your thoughts, feelings, and experiences.

Understanding the Hidden Messages in Your Dreams

Dreams often speak in a language of symbols, like a movie your brain directs to help you make sense of your life. These symbols aren't random; they're clues about what's going on in your world. For example, imagine you dream about climbing a huge mountain. That mountain might represent a big goal you're chasing, like a promotion at work or a personal project. The steep climb could reflect the hard work it takes to get there, and reaching the top might symbolize the success you're aiming for. Or maybe you dream about being stuck in a maze, running into dead ends. That could be your mind's way of showing you're feeling lost or unsure about a decision, like choosing a career path or solving a tricky problem.

These dream symbols are like puzzles, and figuring them out can give you a fresh perspective on your challenges. Let's say you're stressed about a work deadline, and you dream of being chased by a bear. That bear might not be a real threat, but it could stand for the pressure you're feeling. By recognizing this, you might realize it's time to break the project into smaller steps or ask for help. Your dreams are your brain's way of waving a flag and saying, "Hey, here's something to think about!"

Dreams and Your Relationships

Dreams can also shine a light on your emotions, especially when it comes to the people in your life. Ever dream about crossing a rickety bridge to reach someone on the other side? That bridge might represent a relationship you're trying to strengthen or a gap you need to close, like reconnecting with a friend you've drifted apart from. On the flip side, a dream about a stormy ocean might reflect some drama or tension in your life, like an argument with a family member or a misunderstanding with a partner. These emotional symbols are your mind's way of helping you process feelings and find ways to fix things.

For example, if you dream about a locked door between you and someone you care about, it might mean there's something unsaid or unresolved in that relationship. Thinking about what that door represents could inspire you to have an honest conversation or take steps to rebuild trust. Your dreams are like a personal therapist, offering clues to help you navigate your relationships more clearly and confidently.

How to Use Your Dreams to Solve Problems

Want to tap into this dream magic? It's easier than you think! You know to continue writing in your dream journal and analyzing those dream symbols - Here's one I recommend:

1. **Reflect and Connect**: Spend a few minutes thinking about how your dreams relate to your real-life challenges. For example, if you're stressed about a big presentation and dream about being on stage with no script, it might be a sign to prepare more or boost your confidence. Write down any ideas or solutions that pop up when you think about your dreams—they might surprise you!

By paying attention to your dreams, you're giving your brain a chance to share its wisdom. It's like having a conversation with the smartest part of yourself, the part that sees things you might miss when you're busy with everyday life.

FINDING YOURSELF NAKED: REVEALING THE INNER TRUTH

Finding yourself suddenly naked in public can initially feel mortifying. The rush of embarrassment and vulnerability might quickly turn this experience into a nightmare. However, beneath this immediate discomfort lies a valuable opportunity to address underlying concerns and embrace positive change.

Dreams about being naked in public can help solve problems by clearly indicating areas in your life that need attention. Here's why:

- **Highlighting Vulnerability:** Indicates moments when you're feeling emotionally or socially exposed.
- **Identifying Authenticity:** Suggests a need to acknowledge your true self and discard unnecessary pretenses.
- **Signaling Unpreparedness:** Points to situations where more preparation or confidence-building is required.
- **Encouraging Self-Acceptance:** Prompts you to confront insecurities and accept yourself fully.
- **Prompting Personal Growth:** Serves as a call to action to address fears head-on and emerge stronger.

Viewing your naked dream through a problem-solving lens transforms discomfort into empowerment. Recognizing these bullet points allows you to move confidently into exploring deeper ways to transform other nightmares into opportunities for profound personal insight and growth.

Your dreams are like a hidden treasure chest, packed with ideas and insights to help you tackle life's challenges. Whether you're wrestling with a tough work project, sorting out a disagreement with a friend, or chasing a burst of creative inspiration, your dreams can point the way. All you need is a notebook to capture those nighttime adventures, a solid night's sleep to let your brain do its thing, and a bit of curiosity to unlock the magic. You never know, your next great idea might be waiting in tonight's dream!

In the next chapter, we'll dive into the wild and wonderful world of dream types, from the thrilling adventures of lucid dreams to the spooky shadows of nightmares. Are these dreams messages from your deeper self, your brain's way of making sense of your day, or a mix of both? We'll explore them through a spiritual lens, where they might feel like glimpses into your soul, and an analytical one, where they're like snapshots of your thoughts and experiences. Get ready to discover what your dreams, whether they're epic, scary, or just plain weird, can teach you all about Dream Types.

8

DREAM TYPES

The ideas in this chapter are drawn from a vibrant mix of psychological research, cultural wisdom, and historical insights, carefully pieced together from the works of scientists, psychologists, and dream enthusiasts who've studied the magic of the sleeping mind. These aren't my own creations but a synthesis of knowledge to help you explore the incredible world of dreams. Every night, your brain spins a unique story, from soaring through the clouds to facing shadowy fears. These dreams come in all sorts of flavors, each with its own message about your thoughts, feelings, and life. In this chapter, we'll unpack 20 different types of dreams, whether they're thrilling, spooky, or just plain weird, and discover what they might reveal about you. Get ready to see your nighttime adventures in a whole new light and maybe even find some clues to guide your waking life!

THE MANY FACES OF DREAMS

Your dreams are like a personal movie theater in your mind, playing everything from action-packed adventures to quiet, emotional scenes. Some nights, you're the star of a wild fantasy; others, you're stuck in a stressful loop. Each type of dream has its own vibe, and figuring out what they mean can help you understand what's going on in your head, whether it's a worry, a hope, or a spark of creativity. Scientists tell us that dreams kick into high gear during REM (Rapid Eye Movement) sleep, when your brain is buzzing, sorting through your day's experiences and emotions. But dreams aren't just random noise; they're your mind's way of working through life's big and small moments.

Here, we'll look at 15 different dream types, from the ones that make you feel like a superhero to those that leave you puzzled or rattled. For each one, we'll break down what it feels like, why it might show up, and how it could connect to your life, all in simple terms with examples you can relate to. Whether you're curious about flying dreams or wondering why you keep losing your teeth in your sleep, this chapter will help you make sense of it all. Let's jump into the colorful, crazy world of dream types and uncover what your brain is trying to tell you!

1. Lucid Dreams

- **What They Are:** Lucid dreams are when you know you're dreaming and can sometimes take control, like being the director of your own dream movie. You might fly, explore magical places, or even change the story as it unfolds.
- **Why They Happen:** These dreams happen when your brain becomes partly aware during REM sleep, often triggered by strong emotions, stress, or practicing "reality checks" during the day (like asking, "Am I dreaming?"). They're more common if you're thinking about dreams or trying to have one.
- **What They Might Mean:** Lucid dreams are all about empowerment and creativity. They might pop up when you feel confident or crave control over a chaotic part of your life, like a big decision or a creative project.
- **Example:** Picture yourself deep in a jungle, swatting at branches and unsure why you're even there. Then suddenly, you pause. Something feels off. You realize, *this is a dream.* With that awareness, fear vanishes. You lift off the ground and

fly above the treetops to a shimmering waterfall you didn't notice before. As you float down to the water's edge, you feel in charge, peaceful, and excited—like you can change not just this dream, but maybe your real-life situation too.
- **Takeaway:** Lucid dreams remind you that awareness can change everything. They're a space to face fears, explore desires, and experiment with choices in a safe inner world. If you're feeling stuck or powerless in waking life, lucid dreaming might offer a healing form of rehearsal. To invite more, try writing "Am I dreaming?" during the day and visualizing how you'd rewrite a recent dream. Lucid dreaming is more than fun—it can be a gateway to transformation.

2. Nightmares

- **What They Are:** Nightmares are scary dreams that can wake you up, heart racing, from being chased by a monster or losing someone you love. They're like a horror flick your brain plays, leaving you rattled but relieved it's not real.
- **Why They Happen:** Nightmares often come from stress, anxiety, or trauma, especially during tough times like a breakup or work pressure. They're more vivid during REM sleep when emotions are intense, and things like late-night snacks, medications, or poor sleep can worsen them.
- **What They Might Mean:** These dreams might be your brain processing fears or unresolved issues. A nightmare about being trapped could show you're feeling stuck in a job or relationship you don't like.
- **Example:** You're walking through an unfamiliar house, its hallways dark and narrowing. You hear footsteps behind you but can't see anyone. You try to run, but your feet feel heavy. A door slams shut. You're trapped, and the presence behind you is closer now. You scream, but no sound comes out. You wake with your heart pounding and the sense that something inside you was trying to get out. Later that day, you realize you've

been pushing down a fear—maybe about an illness, a relationship, or something left unsaid.
- **Takeaway:** Nightmares often carry urgent emotional messages. They aren't just about fear—they're about attention. What are you avoiding that needs to be named, faced, or healed? Rather than push nightmares away, write them down. Sit with them. If they repeat or feel overwhelming, consider working with a therapist. Nightmares are the mind's flare gun—telling you something matters.

3. Recurring Dreams

- **What They Are:** Recurring dreams are like a favorite song stuck on repeat—they keep coming back with similar scenes, people, or themes, often feeling like your brain's trying to get your attention.
- **Why They Happen:** These dreams often show up when you're dealing with ongoing stress or something unresolved, like a lingering worry or life change. They're common during transitions, like starting a new job or moving to a new city.
- **What They Might Mean:** They might point to something you're avoiding or a lesson your mind wants you to learn. A recurring dream about missing a deadline could reflect anxiety about keeping up with responsibilities.
- **Example:** Every few weeks, you dream you're racing through a school hallway, late for a test. You're unprepared, can't find your classroom, and the clock is ticking louder with every step. Sometimes it's a math test, sometimes history, but the panic is always the same. You haven't been in school for years, but recently your boss gave you a project you feel unequipped to lead—and suddenly the dream returns.
- **Takeaway:** Recurring dreams show where your growth is stuck. They ask: what haven't you dealt with yet? The repetition isn't a punishment—it's a prompt. Look for themes and emotions that return. These dreams are like a mirror, and

the sooner you face what they reflect, the sooner you can shift the pattern.

4. Prophetic or Precognitive Dreams

- **What They Are:** These dreams feel like they predict the future, like dreaming of a friend's new job before they tell you. They're rare and mysterious, often making you wonder if you've got a sixth sense.
- **Why They Happen:** Some experts think these dreams come from your brain picking up subtle clues you didn't notice while awake, like body language or patterns. Others see them as spiritual connections or just lucky coincidences.
- **What They Might Mean:** They might reflect your intuition working overtime or a deep connection to someone. Dreaming of a car crash could be your mind's way of saying, "Be careful!" based on something you sensed.
- **Example:** You dream that your cousin calls to say she's moving to another state for a new job. It feels ordinary, no big emotional charge. Two days later, she texts: "Big news—I'm relocating!" You haven't talked in weeks. The match isn't exact, but it's close enough to leave you wondering, *How did I know?*
- **Takeaway:** Whether intuition, subconscious pattern recognition, or something spiritual, these dreams highlight how sensitive you are to others and your environment. Rather than trying to predict the future, focus on listening more deeply. Prophetic dreams may not always be literal, but they always say something about how in tune you are with life.

5. Erotic Dreams

- **What They Are:** Erotic dreams involve sexual themes, from flirty encounters to intense scenarios. They can be exciting, awkward, or even a bit uncomfortable, depending on the context.

- **Why They Happen:** These dreams often tie to natural desires, hormones, or emotional closeness. They can pop up during REM sleep when emotions are vivid or after a day filled with attraction, stress, or even a romantic movie.
- **What They Might Mean:** They might reflect unmet desires, a need for connection, or just your brain blowing off steam. A dream about a coworker might not mean you're crushing on them, but could show admiration or tension in your work dynamic.
- **Example:** You dream of having a candlelit dinner with a stranger who feels oddly familiar. The conversation flows effortlessly, the chemistry builds, and by the time you lean in for a kiss, it feels more like an emotional merging than lust. You wake up not aroused but moved, wondering who or what you're truly longing for. Later that day, you realize how emotionally disconnected you've been feeling in your current relationship, or even with yourself.
- **Takeaway:** Erotic dreams aren't always about sex; they're often about intimacy, confidence, and the parts of ourselves we've exiled or silenced. They may point to a need for connection, creative fire, or integration of shadow aspects. Rather than feel shame or confusion, use these dreams to ask: *What am I craving—emotionally, spiritually, or creatively?*

6. Flying Dreams

- **What They Are:** Flying dreams let you soar through the sky, free as a bird, often with a rush of joy or power. They're some of the most thrilling dreams you can have.
- **Why They Happen:** These dreams often show up when you're feeling confident, excited, or craving freedom. They're common during REM sleep when your imagination is in high gear.
- **What They Might Mean:** Flying can symbolize breaking free from limits, like a tough situation, or embracing your

potential. A flying dream might appear when you're pumped about a new opportunity, like a promotion.
- **Example:** You dream of running down a grassy hill and lifting effortlessly into the sky. The higher you go, the smaller your problems seem. You glide over trees, mountains, and oceans, feeling powerful and peaceful. When you wake up, you feel refreshed, like something heavy has lifted. You've been contemplating a big move, a new city, a creative project, and this dream gives you that final inner permission to go for it.
- **Takeaway:** Flying dreams are freedom dreams. They remind you of what's possible when you trust your direction. Spiritually, they may represent your higher self-rising above ego limitations. Let them fuel your real-world courage. Ask: *What area of my life is asking me to rise above fear and take flight?*

7. Falling Dreams

- **What They Are:** In falling dreams, you're plummeting off a cliff, a building, or into nowhere—often waking with a jolt before you hit the ground. They're short but intense.
- **Why They Happen:** These can be triggered by stress, insecurity, or even a physical twitch during sleep (called a hypnic jerk). They often happen in early sleep stages.
- **What They Might Mean:** Falling might reflect a fear of losing control, failing, or letting go. A dream of falling off a ladder could mirror anxiety about a risky project or decision.
- **Example:** You're standing on a bridge when the ground crumbles beneath your feet. You fall, slow at first, then faster. The sky blurs, your stomach lurches, and just before you hit the water below, you wake gasping. It's the same dream you had before moving in with your partner. Looking back, you realize it coincided with every big life leap, change, risk, and vulnerability.
- **Takeaway:** Falling dreams often mirror where we feel unsupported or fearful of the unknown. They ask: *What part of me is terrified to let go?* Grounding practices, emotional

processing, and honest reflection can help. These dreams may jolt you awake, but only because they want you to pay attention to where you feel out of control.

8. Being Chased Dreams

- **What They Are:** These dreams have you running from a pursuer—maybe a person, animal, or shadowy figure. They're stressful and make your heart race.
- **Why They Happen:** Chased dreams often stem from anxiety or avoidance, like dodging a problem or responsibility. They're common during stressful times, like exams or conflicts.
- **What They Might Mean:** The pursuer might represent something you're avoiding, like a tough conversation or fear of failure. It's your brain saying, "Time to face this!"
- **Example:** You're sprinting down a forest path, a dark shape just behind you. You don't know who or what it is, you just know you can't let it catch you. You run until the trees blur, your breath shortens, and suddenly, you're cornered. You turn—and the figure vanishes. You wake up shaking. Later, you realize you've been avoiding a hard talk with someone close. The dream wasn't about being hunted. It was about not wanting to confront something painful.
- **Takeaway:** Chased dreams are about confrontation, not escape. They ask: *What am I running from—emotionally, practically, or spiritually?* Once you face the fear behind the dream, the pursuit often stops. These dreams are more than adrenaline—they're opportunities for courage and closure.

9. Teeth Falling Out Dreams

- **What They Are:** These unsettling dreams involve your teeth crumbling, falling out, or breaking, often feeling vivid and alarming, like a bad trip to the dentist.

- **Why They Happen:** They're linked to anxiety about appearance, communication, or aging. Physical sensations, like grinding your teeth, can also trigger them.
- **What They Might Mean:** These dreams might reflect insecurity about how others see you or fear of losing something: confidence, youth, status, or control. They can also point to trouble expressing yourself.
- **Example:** You're at a wedding, mid-toast, raising a glass to speak. As the words leave your mouth, your front teeth crack and fall onto the table. Laughter turns into gasps. You cover your face and run. Waking up, the shame lingers. You remember a meeting yesterday where you felt dismissed after voicing your opinion, and now realize your dream echoed the sting of not being heard.
- **Takeaway:** Teeth dreams are about personal power and visibility. They often show up when you feel like your voice is breaking down or your sense of control is slipping. Spiritually, they can reflect identity shifts: what's being lost to reveal something more authentic? They ask: *Where do I need to speak up, show up, or stop hiding my discomfort?*

10. Daydreams

- **What They Are:** Daydreams happen when you're awake, letting your mind wander into fun or creative scenarios, like imagining a dream vacation or a perfect date.
- **Why They Happen:** They occur when your mind drifts, often during repetitive or boring tasks, and engages your brain's default mode network (your inner creative engine).
- **What They Might Mean:** Daydreams can reflect your hopes, fears, or hidden desires. Daydreaming about a new job might show ambition or anxiety about your career path.
- **Example:** You're folding laundry when you suddenly imagine yourself speaking confidently onstage, winning over an audience with ease. It's vivid—you can hear your voice echo and feel the pride in your chest. You blink, the dryer buzzes,

and the moment is gone. But it leaves a mark. You realize you've been craving recognition, purpose, and a life less behind-the-scenes.
- **Takeaway:** Daydreams aren't distractions: they're blueprints. They show what your heart is rehearsing for. Rather than brushing them off, write them down. What you envision, especially repeatedly, may be what your soul is steering you toward.

11. Epic Dreams

- **What They Are:** Epic dreams are long, movie-like dreams with a clear storyline, like going on a quest or living in a fantasy world. They feel grand and unforgettable.
- **Why They Happen:** These dreams often occur during deep REM sleep and are usually sparked by strong emotions, major life transitions, or creative momentum.
- **What They Might Mean:** They may reflect your deeper life story, your archetypal roles, spiritual path, or biggest internal battles. These dreams aren't just symbolic. They're mythic.
- **Example:** You dream of trekking through a frozen landscape to retrieve a glowing stone from a mountain guarded by wolves. Along the way, you meet mentors, face challenges, and grow braver. The dream spans hours and wakes you with tears, not of fear, but of awe. You feel like you've lived through something sacred.
- **Takeaway:** Epic dreams are soul messages. They carry themes of transformation, purpose, and inner strength. Don't dismiss them as just "weird" or "long." They may be revealing the storyline of your soul's development, especially if they feel like chapters in a larger unfolding journey. Write them down. Revisit them. They may carry truths your waking mind hasn't yet understood.

12. Colorful Dreams

- **What They Are:** These dreams are bursting with vivid colors, sometimes brighter than real life, making scenes like sunsets or forests feel super intense.
- **Why They Happen:** Color-rich dreams often occur when emotions are heightened or creativity is flowing. Sensory experiences may also influence them before sleep.
- **What They Might Mean:** Color can symbolize mood, energy, and emotion. Bright hues may reflect joy, inspiration, or spiritual connection.
- **Example:** You dream of walking through a glowing meadow filled with flowers that pulse with neon light. A purple fox speaks to you in a golden voice. You wake up feeling like you stepped out of a sacred painting. The dream doesn't make "logical" sense, but it stirs something deep—your longing for beauty, magic, and meaning.
- **Takeaway:** Colorful dreams awaken your creative and emotional intelligence. Don't just analyze them: *feel* them. Ask yourself: *What emotion did that color evoke?* These dreams often show you where joy, awe, or wonder are ready to return.

13. Black and White Dreams

- **What They Are:** These dreams lack color, appearing in shades of gray, often feeling stark or muted compared to vivid, colorful dreams.
- **Why They Happen:** They may appear during times of emotional numbness, fatigue, or disconnection. They can also signal reflection, nostalgia, or depression.
- **What They Might Mean:** A black-and-white dream may reflect monotony, sadness, or a life phase lacking vibrancy or clarity.
- **Example:** You dream of walking through an empty town where everything is grayscale. The sky, the buildings, even the people have no color. You feel like a ghost drifting through

someone else's memory. When you wake, you realize you've been on autopilot for weeks: working, cleaning, scrolling, but barely *feeling.*
- **Takeaway:** These dreams are subtle emotional messengers. They may be signaling emotional fatigue or the need to reintroduce joy. Ask: *What area of my life feels drained of color, connection, or presence?* Black-and-white dreams don't mean you're broken—they mean your heart is whispering, *Come back to yourself.*

14. Dreams of the Dead

- **What They Are:** These dreams involve meeting or talking with loved ones who've passed away, often feeling so real you wake up emotional or comforted.
- **Why They Happen:** They're common during periods of grief, transition, or when you're longing for support or closure.
- **What They Might Mean:** These dreams may offer healing, guidance, or connection. Whether symbolic or spiritual, they carry deep emotional weight.
- **Example:** You dream of sitting on a porch beside your late father, watching the stars in silence. He hands you a notebook and says, "You already know what to write." When you wake, your eyes are wet. You've been stuck creatively for months, and the dream feels like a push to begin again.
- **Takeaway:** These dreams are sacred. They may reflect your desire for reconnection, or they may *be* reconnection, depending on your beliefs. Either way, they offer a balm to grief. Honor them by writing them down. Ask what the loved one represented in your life and what part of that you need to call back into your heart.

15. Healing Dreams

- **What They Are:** Healing dreams feel soothing or transformative, often helping you work through emotional or physical pain, like dreaming of being cared for or finding peace.
- **Why They Happen:** These often show up during recovery, after a breakup, a trauma, or during illness, as the mind and spirit seek restoration.
- **What They Might Mean:** They often reflect the beginning of emotional integration or a return to inner balance.
- **Example:** You dream of lying in a field of soft moss while warm sunlight pours over you. An old friend gently places a hand on your heart. No words are spoken, but you feel your chest unclench for the first time in months. You wake up with a quiet strength you didn't know you had.

Takeaway: Healing dreams are like inner rituals. They restore what life or loss has fractured. Let them remind you that healing isn't just about fixing; it's about resting, receiving, and trusting your own timeline. Ask: *What part of me is ready to soften? What part of me finally feels safe?*

WRAPPING IT UP: YOUR DREAMS, YOUR STORY

Your dreams are like a scrapbook of your mind, each type capturing a different piece of who you are: your fears, your hopes, your creativity, and everything in between. Whether you're flying high in a joyful dream, wrestling with a nightmare, or chatting with a loved one from the past, your brain is weaving a story that's uniquely yours. By noticing these dream types, you can start to uncover what's on your mind, whether it's a stress to tackle, a goal to chase, or a memory to hold close. Grab a notebook to jot down your dreams, ensure you're getting plenty of sleep to fuel those REM cycles, and let your nighttime adventures guide you. Your dreams might just point you toward a brighter, more inspired life.

In the next chapter, we'll explore how to dig deeper into these dream types, looking at them through both spiritual and analytical lenses. Are your dreams messages from your heart, your brain making sense of your day, or a bit of both? Get ready to unlock even more secrets about what your dreams mean and how they can light the way forward.

9

SPIRITUAL DIMENSIONS OF DREAMS

The insights in this chapter blend psychological wisdom, spiritual traditions, and stories from dreamers across time, woven together to illuminate the mysteries of your sleeping mind. Every night, your dreams pull you into a world of wonder; sometimes soaring, sometimes unsettling, always deeply personal. In Chapter 8, we explored different dream types, from lucid adventures to haunting nightmares. But some dreams linger not because they scare us, but because they hum with a presence: a message we can't quite grasp.

Take my own story: when I was eight, just days after my brother passed, I lay in bed and saw a gray, smoky figure drift across the ceiling. It wasn't frightening, it felt gentle, almost like it had something to say. My sister stirred and screamed at the same moment, as if she saw it too. My heart raced as my mother held me, whispering, "You're safe." That figure never faded from my memory, not as a nightmare, but as a quiet mystery. Was it grief? Imagination? Or my brother's way of saying goodbye? That moment planted a seed for why I believe dreams can carry spiritual weight.

In this chapter, we'll dive deeper, exploring dreams through two lenses:

- **A spiritual lens**, where dreams might be whispers from the soul, messages from ancestors, or signs from the universe.
- **An analytical lens**, where dreams are your brain sorting emotions, memories, and experiences.

Both lenses are powerful, and you don't have to choose just one. Together, they can help you uncover the hidden treasures in your dreams, whether you're a dreamer who feels the magic or someone who loves a good explanation.

SPIRITUAL DREAM INTERPRETATIONS ACROSS CULTURES

For millennia, humans have turned to dreams for spiritual insight, healing, and connection to something greater. Here's how different traditions have seen dreams as sacred:

- **Ancient Civilizations**: In ancient Egypt, dreams were messages from the gods. People slept in dream temples to seek healing or prophecy. In Greece, the sick visited Asclepian sanctuaries, dreaming of cures from the god Asclepius. Mesopotamians consulted dream priests, believing dreams carried divine warnings or blessings.
- **Eastern Traditions**: Hinduism views dreams as reflections of karma or prophetic glimpses—some texts classify dreams by their spiritual significance. Buddhism sees dreams as illusions but also as potential windows into one's spiritual state. Taoism interprets dreams as signs of yin-yang balance or imbalance.
- **Abrahamic Religions**: In Judaism, Christianity, and Islam, dreams often carry divine weight. Think of Joseph's prophetic dreams in Genesis or the Prophet Muhammad's visions in the Quran—both seen as God's voice breaking through sleep.

- **Indigenous and Shamanic Traditions**: Many Native American tribes view dreams as soul journeys, where ancestors or spirit animals offer guidance. Dreamcatchers filter out bad dreams, letting sacred ones through. In shamanic practices, dreams are portals to other worlds, rich with meaning.
- **Modern Spirituality**: New Age and transpersonal movements see dreams as pathways to the collective unconscious or personal growth, often exploring lucid dreaming or astral projection as spiritual tools.

These traditions show dreams aren't just random; they're bridges to the unseen, shaped by culture and belief.

The Spiritual Lens: Dreams as Sacred Experiences

What if your dreams are more than fleeting images? What if they're letters from your soul, carrying guidance or glimpses of the divine? Through a spiritual lens, dreams become sacred, a space where your higher self, spirit guides, or the universe might speak. This approach asks you to meet your dreams with reverence and curiosity.

To start, set an intention before sleep: "Show me what I need to know" or "Guide me toward peace." Light a candle, meditate, or whisper a prayer to invite spiritual dreams. When you wake, jot down symbols, feelings, or any sense of presence. Over time, you might spot patterns, like recurring animals or lights, that feel meaningful.

Here are some common spiritual dream symbols to ponder:

- **Light**: A sign of divine presence, enlightenment, or awakening.
- **Water**: Purification, emotional flow, or the unconscious rising.
- **Animals**: Spirit guides or totems reflecting qualities like strength (a bear) or intuition (an owl).
- **Numbers**: Sacred messages, like "3" for harmony or "7" for spiritual growth.

- **Deceased Loved Ones**: Visitations offering comfort or wisdom.

These aren't fixed meanings—trust your intuition to decode what resonates for you.

THE ANALYTICAL LENS: PSYCHOLOGICAL THEORIES OF DREAMING

While the spiritual lens invites us to see dreams as sacred, the analytical lens grounds us in science and psychology. Let's explore key theories that explain why we dream and what dreams might mean:

- **Freud's Psychoanalytic Theory**: Sigmund Freud, the father of psychoanalysis, saw dreams as "the royal road to the unconscious." He believed dreams reveal repressed desires, often sexual or aggressive, disguised in symbols. For example, dreaming of a snake might symbolize repressed sexual energy. While controversial, Freud's work opened the door to dream analysis as a tool for self-discovery (Freud, 1900).
- **Jung's Archetypes and the Collective Unconscious**: Carl Jung, Freud's student, took a broader view. He saw dreams as messages from the unconscious, often featuring universal symbols or "archetypes" like the Hero or the Shadow. Jung believed dreams help us integrate parts of ourselves we've ignored, guiding us toward wholeness (Jung, 1964).
- **Cognitive Theories**: Modern psychologists view dreams as a way to process emotions, solve problems, or simulate threats. For instance, the "threat simulation theory" suggests nightmares help us rehearse danger, boosting survival (Revonsuo, 2000). Cognitive theories also link dreaming to memory consolidation, with studies showing that REM sleep enhances learning (Walker, 2017).
- **Neuroscientific Perspectives**: Neuroscience reveals that dreaming occurs during REM sleep, when the brain's emotional centers are active, but logic centers are quiet. This

explains why dreams feel vivid yet bizarre. Research also shows that dreaming may help regulate emotions, with dream content often reflecting our waking concerns (Cartwright, 2010).

These theories offer a scientific counterpoint to spiritual views, showing how dreams might serve practical functions in our mental and emotional lives.

INTERPRETING SPECIFIC DREAM TYPES: SPIRITUAL AND ANALYTICAL INSIGHTS

Let's explore six dream types—lucid dreams, nightmares, flying dreams, teeth falling out dreams, dreams of the dead, and prophetic dreams—through both lenses. Each offers a unique window into your inner world.

Lucid Dreams

- **Spiritual Lens**: Lucid dreams, where you're aware and in control, might be gateways to higher consciousness. Some traditions see them as chances to meet spirit guides or glimpse your soul's purpose.
- **Analytical Lens**: These reflect your brain's creativity, often tied to confidence or problem-solving—like rehearsing a big decision.
- **Example**: You lucidly explore a glowing temple. Spiritually, it's your soul seeking wisdom. Analytically, it's your mind celebrating a breakthrough.
- **Try This**: Journal the dream and ask, "What felt sacred?" Meditate on its message or tackle a challenge it highlights.

Nightmares

- **Spiritual Lens**: A nightmare, like being chased, might be a spiritual test—your soul urging you to face fear or heal a shadow.
- **Analytical Lens**: It's stress bubbling up, like anxiety over a deadline, pushing you to act.
- **Example**: A shadowy figure pursues you. Spiritually, it's a call to confront doubt. Analytically, it's unresolved tension.
- **Try This**: Write what scared you and pray for courage—or list steps to ease the stress.

Flying Dreams

- **Spiritual Lens**: Soaring skyward might be your soul craving freedom or signaling astral travel—a divine push to rise above.
- **Analytical Lens**: It's confidence or escape, tied to a win or a need for a break.
- **Example**: You glide over mountains. Spiritually, it's a nudge to chase a passion. Analytically, it's joy from success.
- **Try This**: Ask, "What lifts me up?" Visualize it spiritually or plan a freeing activity.

Teeth Falling Out Dreams

- **Spiritual Lens**: Losing teeth might mean shedding old ways or speaking your truth—a soulful release.
- **Analytical Lens**: It's insecurity about looks or words, like fearing judgment.
- **Example**: Teeth crumble mid-conversation. Spiritually, it's about authenticity. Analytically, it's social worry.
- **Try This**: Reflect on "What's unsaid?" Meditate on honesty or rehearse a tough talk.

Dreams of the Dead

- **Spiritual Lens**: These can feel like visitations—loved one's crossing the veil to guide or comfort.
- **Analytical Lens**: It's your mind processing grief or longing, seeking closure.
- **Example**: A late grandparent smiles at you. Spiritually, it's their spirit checking in. Analytically, it's memory at work.
- **Try This**: Note their message and light a candle—or write them a letter.

Prophetic Dreams

- **Spiritual Lens**: Dreams hinting at the future might be divine nudges, like a warning or blessing.
- **Analytical Lens**: Your brain's piecing together subtle cues, like intuition in overdrive.
- **Example**: You foresee a friend's joy. Spiritually, it's a cosmic heads-up. Analytically, it's pattern recognition.
- **Try This**: Track if it comes true, then meditate on its purpose—or analyze what sparked it.

Case Studies: Dream Interpretation in Action

Let's see how these lenses apply to real dreams:

Case Study 1: Sarah's Flying Dream

Sarah, 32, dreamed of flying over a golden city. She felt free and joyful.

- **Spiritual Interpretation**: Her soul yearns for freedom, urging her to chase a passion like travel.
- **Analytical Interpretation**: She recently got a promotion, and her brain's celebrating success.

Insight: Both lenses highlight joy and potential—spiritually, it's a call to adventure; analytically, it's confidence.

Case Study 2: Mark's Nightmare

Mark, 45, dreamed of being trapped in a dark forest. He woke anxious.

- **Spiritual Interpretation**: His soul's pushing him to face a fear, like leaving a toxic job.
- **Analytical Interpretation**: He's stressed about work deadlines, and his brain's signaling overwhelm.

Insight: Both suggest action—spiritually, to confront fear; analytically, to manage stress.

Case Study 3: Emma's Dream of Her Late Mother

Emma, 28, dreamed her mother, who passed last year, hugged her and said, "I'm proud."

- **Spiritual Interpretation**: A visitation offering comfort and closure.
- **Analytical Interpretation**: Her mind's processing grief, creating a sense of peace.

Insight: Both bring healing—spiritually, through connection; analytically, through emotional release.

These cases show how both lenses can enrich your understanding, offering complementary insights.

ADDRESSING CRITICISMS OF DREAM INTERPRETATION

Dream interpretation isn't without its skeptics. Here are common critiques and balanced responses:

- **Criticism 1: Lack of Scientific Evidence**
    - Some argue that dream interpretation, especially spiritual views, lacks empirical support. While it's true that spiritual beliefs can't be "proven," research does show that dreams reflect waking concerns and can aid emotional processing (Cartwright, 2010). Both lenses have value—science for understanding mechanisms, spirituality for meaning.
- **Criticism 2: Subjectivity**
    - Interpretations can feel arbitrary, varying widely. This is valid, but subjectivity is part of human experience. Tools like journaling or group sharing can help refine insights. Jung himself said, "The dream is its own interpretation" (Jung, 1964)—meaning your personal resonance matters most.
- **Criticism 3: Overemphasis on Symbolism**
    - Critics say focusing on symbols ignores dreams' randomness. Yet, studies show that dreams often incorporate waking themes (Domhoff, 2003). Symbols, whether spiritual or psychological, can be useful if they resonate with you.

Ultimately, dream interpretation is a personal journey. Use what feels true to you and let go of what doesn't.

Practical Tools for Spiritual Dream Work

Here's how to dive into your dreams' spiritual side with simple, adaptable practices:

1. **Dream Incubation Ritual**
    - Pick a question (e.g., "What's my next step?").
    - Write it down, slip it under your pillow.

- Light a candle, say a prayer, or affirm your intent.
- Visualize receiving an answer as you sleep.
- Record your dream and reflect on its hints.
2. **Meditation for Dream Guidance**
   - Before bed, breathe deeply and imagine a light inviting sacred dreams.
   - Repeat, "I welcome wisdom in my dreams."
   - Wake and note any insights.
3. **Spiritual Dream Journaling**
   - Log symbols, emotions, and any "otherworldly" vibes.
   - Ask, "What's my soul saying?"
4. **Dream Altar**
   - Set up a space with meaningful items (crystals, photos).
   - Place your journal there and connect nightly.
5. **Dream Sharing Circle**
   - Share dreams with others for collective insight—listen and reflect together.

Integrating Spiritual Dream Insights into Daily Life

Bring your dreams into waking life with these ideas:

- **Creative Expression**: Paint a dream scene or write its story.
- **Meditation Focus**: Use a dream symbol (like water) to deepen reflection.
- **Action Steps**: If a dream urges change, take one small step—like calling a friend it featured.
- **Community**: Share dreams with a group for support.

Balance is key; use dreams as inspiration, not sole decision-makers.

WRAPPING IT UP: YOUR DREAMS, YOUR LIGHT

These lenses don't clash; they dance. Jung's archetypes echo spiritual symbols, while neuroscience links dreaming to transcendence. A lucid dream might be both a spiritual gift and a mental flex. Embrace both for a fuller picture.

Your dreams are a gift, whether divine whispers or brain sparks, they guide you. A flying dream might ignite a passion, a nightmare might heal a wound. Keep a journal, explore both lenses, and let them shape your days. Sleep boldly, wake curious; your dreams are a compass for a life of meaning and wonder.

As we move forward, we'll begin to explore what some of the world's most influential psychologists, from Freud to Jung to modern neuroscientists, have uncovered about the *why* behind our dreams. In Chapter 10: Psychological Theories, we'll dig into how the mind uses dreams to process emotion, store memory, and sometimes, speak the truths we can't yet say aloud.

Let's dive into the science and psychology of dreaming and discover just how much your sleeping mind is doing for your waking life.

10

DREAM INCUBATION AND CONTROL

WHAT IF YOU COULD ASK YOUR DREAMS FOR HELP?

I magine lying in bed, whispering a question into the dark, and waking up with an answer that shifts everything, a subtle feeling of peace, a new perspective, or even a bold next step. That's the heart of dream incubation: a practice that turns sleep into something sacred. It isn't about forcing your mind to do something mystical. Instead, it's about *inviting* your subconscious to help you with something that matters. It could be a dilemma you can't stop thinking about. It might be grief you haven't found words for yet. Or maybe you're simply longing for inspiration.

Dream incubation is a gentle, purposeful act. Before you fall asleep, you set a clear question in your heart, a quiet call for help or insight. You might not get a loud, dramatic answer, but often, something shifts. A symbol appears. A tone lingers. A sense of knowing takes root.

This practice is ancient. In sacred healing temples of Ancient Greece, seekers slept on stone beds, asking for dreams that would bring guidance. In Indigenous traditions worldwide, people have long believed dreams carry messages from ancestors, spirits, or nature itself.

Today, dream researchers and therapists acknowledge that our dreams often reflect exactly what we need to see if we ask the right questions.

What's beautiful about dream incubation is that anyone can do it. You don't need to meditate for hours, interpret symbols like an expert, or have a spiritual awakening. You only need to care. To ask something real. To mean it.

When you incubate a dream, you're not performing magic. You're planting a seed. You're saying to the deepest part of yourself: "Please help me understand this." And often, your dreams will respond.

WHY DREAM INCUBATION WORKS

While we sleep, our minds remain highly active. In fact, sleep is one of the most creatively and emotionally productive times for the human brain. During the night, especially in REM sleep, the brain isn't resting; it's working in an entirely different mode, making associations, clearing clutter, and sorting through emotions. This is when the mind processes unresolved feelings, stores memories, integrates new experiences, and solves problems in ways that aren't always possible when we're awake.

Dream incubation works by giving this incredibly powerful subconscious process a specific task to focus on. Instead of letting your mind wander freely through scattered thoughts, you're offering it a gentle prompt: a heartfelt question or emotional dilemma. It's like sending a memo to your inner world saying, "Work on this tonight."

From a psychological perspective, this approach is grounded in how the brain operates. Studies in neuroscience have shown that REM sleep enhances creativity, problem-solving, and emotional processing. It's why we often wake with new insights or feel emotionally lighter after a night of dreaming. Dream incubation leverages these brain functions, aligning them with conscious intention. You're not forcing anything; you're simply guiding your natural mental activity toward a meaningful direction.

On an emotional level, dreams are a way for us to express what we can't always articulate during the day. When you give your dreams a specific concern to address, whether it's grief, confusion, or curiosity, your subconscious uses symbols, metaphors, and emotional imagery to bring clarity or comfort. It's the language of the soul and psyche, working through visuals, feelings, and subtle messages that your waking mind can begin to interpret.

Spiritually, many people believe that dream incubation opens a door to inner guidance, a higher power, or the wisdom of the universe. Whether you view this as divine communication, ancestral connection, or a deepened relationship with your own soul, incubation creates space for something sacred to emerge. You are setting a quiet intention and trusting that something beyond logic may offer an answer.

Think of your subconscious as a creative problem-solver working behind the scenes. When you go to bed with a clear, emotionally charged question, it's like giving that inner worker a thoughtful assignment. Your mind might not deliver a perfectly clear answer, but it often offers symbols, metaphors, emotional landscapes, or dream narratives that mirror the truth you're seeking. Even a single image: a locked door, a soaring bird, a familiar face, can hold a profound message.

Most importantly, the subconscious responds to suggestion. The key is to be clear, sincere, and patient. If you approach dream incubation like a gentle conversation rather than a demand, your inner world is more likely to respond. Trust the process. Trust yourself. The answers often unfold not all at once, but in layers, one dream at a time.

How to Incubate a Dream

Dream incubation is a deeply personal and surprisingly simple practice that anyone can do, no special tools, rituals, or prior experience required. All it takes is a sincere question and a willingness to listen to your inner wisdom. What matters most is your emotional investment in the question you're asking. Here's a clear, step-by-step guide crafted for the average reader—easy to follow, yet powerful in its impact.

Step 1: Choose a Clear, Meaningful Question

Start by selecting a question that truly matters to you. It should be specific, emotionally relevant, and open-ended to invite insight from your subconscious. Avoid vague questions like "What's the meaning of life?" and instead focus on something personal and actionable. Here are examples across different life areas and emotional challenges to inspire you:

- **Career and Work:**
    - "What steps can I take to advance in my current job?"
    - "How can I find more fulfillment and purpose in my work?"
    - "What career path aligns best with my passions and skills?"
- **Relationships:**
    - "What can I do to improve communication with my partner?"
    - "How can I resolve the ongoing conflict with my friend or family member?"
    - "What do I need to understand about my role in this relationship?"
- **Personal Growth:**
    - "What is holding me back from reaching my full potential?"
    - "How can I cultivate more self-compassion and self-love?"
    - "What new habit or practice would most benefit my personal development?"
- **Health and Well-being:**
    - "What lifestyle changes can I make to improve my energy levels?"
    - "How can I better manage my stress and anxiety?"
    - "What does my body need right now to heal and thrive?"
- **Emotional Challenges:**
    - *Anxiety:* "What is the root cause of my anxiety, and how can I address it?"

- *Grief:* "How can I honor my loved one's memory while finding peace?"
- *Self-Doubt:* "What strengths do I possess that I can rely on to overcome my doubts?"

Pick a question that resonates deeply, or use these as a starting point to craft your own. The more heartfelt and honest your question, the more likely your subconscious will respond.

Step 2: Write It Down

Write your question on a piece of paper or in a notebook and keep it by your bedside. This simple act anchors your intention, making it tangible and signaling to your inner mind that you're serious about seeking an answer.

Step 3: Create a Quiet, Supportive Sleep Environment

Before bed, take a few minutes to calm your mind and body. Turn off screens an hour before sleep, dim the lights, sip herbal tea, or play soft music. A peaceful setting tells your body it's safe to turn inward. You might light a candle, hold a meaningful object (like a crystal or photo), or take three slow, deep breaths as a mini ritual.

Step 4: Set the Intention as You Fall Asleep

As you lie in bed, gently repeat your question to yourself a few times —either aloud or silently. To strengthen your intention, try one or more of these optional techniques:

- **Visualization:** Picture writing your question on a piece of paper and placing it in a special box or envelope. Imagine sealing it and trusting your subconscious to work on it overnight. Or envision a wise figure—a guide or mentor—who will help reveal the answer in your dream.
- **Affirmation:** Repeat a positive statement like, "I am open to receiving clear and helpful guidance from my dreams tonight," or "My subconscious holds the answers I seek." Say it a few times to reinforce your focus.

- **Sensory Cue:** Light a scented candle, dab on a drop of essential oil (like lavender), or play gentle music or nature sounds. Link this scent or sound to your question, creating a signal for your mind to tune in.

After setting your intention, stay curious and trusting—don't force it. Let yourself drift into sleep, knowing your inner world is listening.

Step 5: Sleep and Let Go

Once your intention is set, release any need to control the outcome. Don't overthink or try to steer the dream. Your subconscious thrives on freedom, so let it take over as you slip into sleep's natural flow.

Step 6: Record the Dream Immediately Upon Waking

The moment you wake up—even if it's the middle of the night or just a fleeting fragment—write down what you remember. Jot down images, emotions, colors, or words. Don't dismiss anything as random; these details often carry hidden meaning.

Step 7: Reflect on the Dream's Message

Later, revisit your notes. Reflect with these questions:

- What stands out emotionally?
- Are there patterns or symbols?
- How might this relate to my question?
- Dreams rarely offer direct answers but speak through metaphor and feeling. If you asked about change and dreamed of a river, or sought confidence and saw a lion, trust your intuition to connect the dots.

Over time, this practice can make your dreams more vivid and responsive. You're not just chasing answers—you're building a bridge to your inner wisdom, one dream at a time.

UNDERSTANDING THE DREAM'S RESPONSE

Dreams speak in the language of metaphor, emotion, and symbol. They rarely give straightforward answers, but that doesn't mean they aren't answering. Let's say you ask your dream, "How can I move forward from this heartbreak?" and you dream of being in a stormy sea that eventually calms as you reach a sunny shore. While that may seem like a simple image, it reflects an emotional journey—turmoil giving way to peace. That's your answer, even if it isn't spelled out in words.

When reviewing a dream, ask yourself:

- What part of the dream stood out the most?
- How did I feel during and after the dream?
- What does the imagery remind me of in my waking life?

Your dream might show you a locked door when you're feeling stuck, or a baby animal when you're nurturing a new idea. It may even replay a memory from a different angle, highlighting something you missed. The key is to stay open, intuitive, and non-judgmental. Insight often comes when you're not forcing it.

COMMON DREAM SYMBOLS DURING INCUBATION

Dream symbols can feel like riddles wrapped in emotion, but they often point directly to what's stirring in your inner world. When you practice dream incubation, your subconscious may respond with powerful visuals that speak volumes, even when they're wrapped in mystery. Some symbols are universal enough to show up for many people, but the way you interpret them will always be personal. Still, it's fun to see what tends to appear when we ask our dreams for help.

Here are a few common, and a few delightfully unexpected, symbols you might see in your incubation dreams:

- **Doors:** These are classic dream symbols. A closed door may suggest a blocked opportunity, while an open one might be a sign of new beginnings or permission to move forward. Multiple doors? Choices, options, or indecision.
- **Storms:** Storms often show up when there's emotional intensity brewing inside. Think of them as emotional weather reports from your soul. A passing storm might suggest healing is in motion. A never-ending one? You may need to address unresolved conflict or inner turmoil.
- **Animals:** These are messengers from your instinctual self. A lion might show up when you need courage. A snake could represent fear, transformation, or healing (yes, it can mean all three!). A butterfly? Change is coming.
- **Children or Babies:** These often symbolize vulnerability, your inner child, or something new being born in your life: an idea, a hope, or even a relationship.
- **Bridges:** Bridges tend to symbolize transitions. Are you stuck halfway across? Maybe you're in between stages. Are you leaping to the other side? It could be time to take a risk.
- **Elevators and Stairs:** Going up often represents growth or spiritual elevation. Going down might signal introspection or returning to something buried. Stuck between floors? That might say something about feeling trapped or suspended between choices.
- **Flying or Floating:** These are joyful symbols: freedom, release, perspective. If you're flying effortlessly, your spirit might be soaring. Struggling to take off? Something could be weighing you down.
- **Phones, Texts, or Letters:** These are communication symbols. If someone is trying to reach you, ask yourself: what message am I not hearing, or what truth am I avoiding?
- **Clothing or Being Naked:** Clothing often symbolizes identity. Are you overdressed? Maybe you're hiding

something. Are you naked in public? It could reflect a fear of vulnerability or feeling exposed.

And of course, dream symbols can be totally quirky, random, and weird. A dancing octopus? That might be your creativity asking for some freedom. A talking tree? Maybe your roots want attention. Trust your gut. You'll know when a symbol strikes a chord, even if it doesn't make logical sense.

Bottom line: The meaning lives in *your* connection to the symbol. One person's snake is fear. Another's is rebirth. Pay attention to how you feel in the dream. That's usually the biggest clue.

And remember, it's not about solving the puzzle perfectly. It's about starting a conversation with your inner world.

Addressing Specific Emotional and Psychological Challenges through Dream Incubation

While Chapter 10, "Dream Incubation and Control," introduces the foundational techniques of dream incubation, it currently focuses on general methods without exploring how this practice can address specific emotional or psychological needs. To enhance its practical value, this section expands the chapter by applying dream incubation to targeted challenges—grief, anxiety, trauma, and creativity. Each area includes tailored questions to set intentions, visualizations to guide the subconscious, and reflections to integrate dream insights, making the practice actionable for readers seeking support through their dreams.

Dream Incubation: A Tool for Targeted Exploration

Dream incubation involves setting an intention before sleep to guide your dreams toward a specific focus. While the general techniques outlined earlier in this chapter provide a strong starting point, applying them to particular issues can unlock deeper insights and healing. Below, we explore how to adapt dream incubation for four common challenges, offering practical steps to make your dreamwork more purposeful and impactful.

Dream Incubation for Grief

Why It Helps: Grief often leaves us with lingering emotions or unfinished conversations. Dreams can serve as a gentle space to process loss, reconnect with what we've lost, or find solace.

Tailored Questions:

- What do I miss most about who or what I've lost?
- If I could speak to them one last time, what would I say?
- What memory of them feels most comforting?

Visualization: As you drift to sleep, picture a peaceful setting—a quiet meadow, a cozy room, or a calm shoreline. Imagine the person or thing you're grieving appearing in this space. See them clearly, and let the scene unfold naturally—perhaps you share a moment of silence, a conversation, or a warm embrace.

Reflection:

- Did the dream offer comfort or a new perspective on my grief?
- What emotions or images stood out?
- How can I carry any sense of peace from the dream into my day?

Dream Incubation for Anxiety

Why It Helps: Anxiety can feel overwhelming, but dreams can reveal its roots or offer a sense of calm that's hard to access when awake. Incubating dreams for anxiety invites your subconscious to explore solutions or soothing imagery.

Tailored Questions:

- What would it feel like to let go of my worries?
- Where do I feel safest and most at peace?
- What's one anxious thought I'd like clarity on?

Visualization: Before bed, envision a safe haven—a tranquil forest, a warm bed, or a protective circle of light. Picture yourself resting there, joined by a calming presence (a friend, a pet, or even an abstract figure of peace). Let this presence ease your mind as you fall asleep.

Reflection:

- Did the dream shed light on my anxiety or its source?
- What calming elements appeared that I can revisit?
- How might I bring the dream's tranquility into my waking life?

Dream Incubation for Trauma

Why It Helps: Trauma can echo in our minds and dreams, but incubating dreams with a focus on healing can foster empowerment and safety. This approach requires caution to avoid re-traumatization, emphasizing gentle exploration over confrontation.

Tailored Questions:

- What does healing mean to me right now?
- What symbol or person represents strength and support?
- What small piece of my trauma am I ready to face or release?

Visualization: Imagine a symbol of resilience—a sturdy tree, a glowing light, or a guardian figure. See it enveloping you in safety and warmth. If comfortable, visualize yourself taking a small, empowered step, like setting down a burden or standing tall.

Reflection:

- How did the dream feel—safe, challenging, or something else?
- What images or messages might aid my healing?
- What's one kind action I can take for myself based on the dream?

Note: Trauma is complex, and dream incubation isn't a replacement for professional support. Pair this practice with therapy if needed, and proceed with self-compassion.

Dream Incubation for Creativity

Why It Helps: The subconscious is a treasure trove of inspiration. By incubating dreams for creativity, you can tap into fresh ideas, solve problems, or ignite your imagination for projects.

Tailored Questions:

- What creative challenge do I want to explore?
- What excites me most about this project or idea?
- If my creativity had a voice, what would it tell me?

Visualization: Picture yourself in a vibrant creative space—a painter's studio, a writer's desk, or a boundless dreamscape. See your tools or project before you and imagine your ideas flowing effortlessly as you begin to work.

Reflection:

- Did the dream spark new ideas or approaches?
- What images or feelings can fuel my creative process?
- How can I weave the dream's inspiration into my work?

Making It Work for You

To apply these techniques:

- **Set Your Intention**: Before sleep, focus on one question or phrase (e.g., "Show me a path through my anxiety").
- **Relax**: Use deep breathing or a soothing ritual to prepare your mind.
- **Record Your Dreams**: Keep a journal handy to capture insights upon waking.

This section enhances Chapter 10 by applying dream incubation techniques to address specific emotional and psychological challenges: grief, anxiety, trauma, and creativity. For each issue, it provides tailored questions, visualizations, and reflections to guide the process, making dream incubation a practical and targeted tool for personal growth and healing. It emphasizes the importance of setting intentions, relaxing before sleep, and recording dreams upon waking to maximize effectiveness, offering readers actionable support through their dreams.

WHEN NOTHING HAPPENS

Sometimes you set an intention, go to sleep with focus, and wake up with... nothing. No dream. No message. Maybe just fog. That's okay. Dream incubation isn't a vending machine. It's more like sending a message in a bottle and waiting to see when and how the ocean responds.

The most effective guidance is to remain calm and make another attempt. Keep the question alive in your heart. Return to it the next night. Try writing it again, maybe worded slightly differently. Avoid screens before bed, as they disrupt the connection to the dream world. Keep a dream journal close and write down even small fragments. Sometimes the message comes in a whisper, or across several nights.

Dream incubation is a reminder that you are not just a passive receiver of dreams. You are a participant. When you approach your dream life with intention and respect, it often responds with surprising depth.

Asking your dreams for insight can become a quiet nightly ritual, a doorway to deeper connection with yourself. Whether or not a simple answer arrives immediately, the act of asking alone can shift something inside you.

So tonight, don't just fall asleep. Ask a question. Set an intention. Invite your dreams to speak. And most importantly, listen.

Because they are listening too.

As we continue this journey, it's time to zoom out and take a look at the bigger picture. In the next chapter, we'll explore what some of the most influential thinkers in psychology, Freud, Jung, and beyond, have to say about dreams. Why does your mind construct these strange, symbolic stories at night? What are they really doing for your emotions, your memory, your healing?

From unconscious desires to archetypal patterns and memory processing, Chapter 12: Psychological Theories will give you a deeper understanding of how the mind uses dreams to make meaning, resolve conflict, and reflect who we truly are beneath the surface.

11

PSYCHOLOGICAL THEORIES – A PERSONAL LENS

Dreams have a rhythm, a depth, and a hidden architecture. They are not just curious nighttime experiences. They are mirrors of memory, longing, emotion, and unresolved fears. In this chapter, we explore psychological theories of dreams, not from the lens of textbooks, but through the dreams that have shown up throughout this book. These dreams are real, emotional, and deeply human. They are the heartbeat of this chapter.

Instead of dissecting Freud and Jung in academic terms, we'll use their insights to understand something far more personal: why your mind brings certain images, patterns, and sensations to the surface at night. Through the dream of the gray figure, the dream of the train engulfed by the mountainside, the maze with no exit, and Reggie the dog with the dangling paw, we'll discover how the psyche communicates and what it wants us to notice, heal, or integrate.

But first, let's ground ourselves in the foundational theories of dream interpretation, starting with Sigmund Freud and Carl Jung, and then expanding into modern perspectives like Gestalt therapy and contemporary neuroscience. These frameworks will help us decode the emotional and symbolic language of dreams, making their messages clearer and more actionable.

FREUD'S THEORY: DREAMS AS WISH FULFILLMENT AND THE UNCONSCIOUS

Sigmund Freud, the father of psychoanalysis, saw dreams as a royal road to the unconscious mind. In his seminal work *The Interpretation of Dreams* (1900), he proposed that dreams are expressions of repressed desires, often rooted in childhood experiences or unresolved conflicts. He distinguished between manifest content—the surface-level storyline of the dream- and latent content, the hidden, symbolic meaning beneath it. For Freud, the unconscious disguises these desires through symbols to shield the dreamer from their raw, often uncomfortable truths.

Central to Freud's theory is the idea of wish fulfillment. Dreams, he argued, allow us to experience what we cannot in waking life, fulfilling desires that might otherwise remain suppressed. Even nightmares, he suggested, could reflect a wish, perhaps a desire for punishment or a way to confront buried fears. The unconscious uses dreams to release tension, offering a safe space for the mind to process what it cannot openly acknowledge.

Applying Freud to the Dream of the Gray Figure

Consider the dream of the gray, smoky figure drifting across the ceiling, which emerged shortly after the death of a sibling. From a Freudian lens, this dream might represent a repressed wish to reconnect with the lost sibling, a longing too painful to face directly in waking life. The manifest content is the drifting figure, vague and silent, while the latent content could be the dreamer's unconscious desire for presence amidst absence. The smokiness suggests something elusive, mirroring how grief can feel both tangible and out of reach.

The shared experience with the sister, who screamed at the same moment, might intrigue Freud as a sign of a family-level unconscious wish—a collective yearning for the sibling's return, manifesting in a synchronized vision. The dream becomes a way to process grief while protecting the dreamer from its full emotional weight, fulfilling a wish for connection in a disguised form.

Jung's Theory: Archetypes, the Collective Unconscious, and Individuation

Carl Jung, once Freud's protégé, took a broader view of dreams. He introduced the collective unconscious, a shared reservoir of human experience populated by archetypes—universal symbols like the Hero, the Shadow, or the Wise Old Man. Unlike Freud's focus on personal desires, Jung saw dreams as messages from the unconscious, guiding us toward individuation: the integration of the conscious and unconscious mind into a whole self.

For Jung, dreams are not merely wish fulfillment; they are compensatory, balancing the psyche by revealing what we've ignored or suppressed. The Shadow, for instance, represents the hidden, often darker aspects of our personality, while other archetypes might offer wisdom or signal transformation. Dreams, in Jung's view, are a dialogue between the ego and the deeper Self.

Applying Jung to the Dream of the Gray Figure

Through a Jungian lens, the gray figure could embody an archetype, perhaps the Shadow or a Psychopomp. The Shadow often appears as an unsettling or vague figure, reflecting unacknowledged emotions like grief or guilt. Here, it might symbolize the dreamer's suppressed sorrow, hovering in the unconscious until it demands attention.

Alternatively, the figure could be a Psychopomp, a guide between worlds, emerging during a time of loss to bridge the conscious mind and the unconscious realm of death. Its gray, smoky nature suggests a liminal state, neither fully present nor absent, much like the grieving process. The shared scream with the sister might hint at a collective unconscious experience, where an archetype resonates across family members touched by the same loss.

THE TRAIN AND THE MOUNTAIN – RESISTANCE, OVERWHELM, AND SUBCONSCIOUS SYMBOLISM

In the dream of a train steadily traversing mountains only to be silently engulfed by the mountainside, we find a rich tableau for interpretation. No violence, no crash—just a quiet surrender to something vast.

Freudian Interpretation

Freud might see the train as the ego, the conscious self driving toward progress or control, while the mountain represents the superego, the internalized rules and pressures that loom large. The engulfment could symbolize a wish to escape these demands, a surrender to the unconscious desire for relief from responsibility. The silence suggests a repressed conflict; progress halted not by force, but by the weight of expectation.

Jungian Interpretation

Jung might interpret this as a transformative encounter. The train, a symbol of personal journey, is absorbed by the mountain, the unconscious, or the collective forces of nature. This isn't destruction but a call to integrate the ego into the larger Self. The dream could urge the dreamer to relinquish rigid control and trust the unconscious process, a step toward individuation where surrender becomes growth.

Contemporary Perspectives: Emotional Shutdown

Modern psychology might frame this as a reflection of emotional overwhelm. The slow, silent engulfment mirrors the experience of shutting down when feelings or pressures become too much. Neuroscience suggests dreams process emotional residue, and this dream could be the mind's way of symbolizing unspoken burdens, inviting release.

The Maze – Repetition, Anxiety, and the Search for Escape

The dream of a maze with no exit is a vivid metaphor for entrapment, a common experience in anxiety or trauma. Let's explore it through multiple lenses.

Freudian Interpretation

For Freud, the maze might represent the unconscious mind's labyrinth of repressed conflicts. The endless paths and dead ends could symbolize defense mechanisms blocking the dreamer from confronting a buried wish or fear. The lack of escape might reflect a wish to remain hidden from painful truths, trapped by the psyche's own protections.

Jungian Interpretation

Jung would likely see the maze as a journey of individuation. Each turn and dead end is an aspect of the self, emotions, traits, or memories, awaiting integration. The maze isn't a prison but a process, urging the dreamer to persist in self-discovery despite disorientation. It's a call to face the unconscious, step by step.

Gestalt Therapy: The Maze as the Self

In Gestalt therapy, pioneered by Fritz Perls, every dream element is a part of the dreamer. The maze isn't external; it *is* the dreamer. The walls might represent resistance, the paths indecision, and the dead ends suppressed feelings. This approach invites the dreamer to dialogue with these parts, integrating them to find inner harmony.

Contemporary Research: Problem-Solving and Anxiety

Modern dream research highlights dreams' role in emotional regulation and problem-solving. A maze dream could be the brain rehearsing solutions to waking-life confusion or anxiety, testing pathways in a safe space. The emotional tone, panic, or frustration points to areas of life where the dreamer feels stuck.

Reggie and the Dangling Paw – Vulnerability, Empathy, and Attachment

The dream of Reggie, the dog with the injured paw, carries an immediate emotional pull. The dreamer doesn't analyze him—she feels him, frozen in compassion.

Freudian Interpretation

Freud might view Reggie as a symbol of repressed vulnerability, perhaps a childhood wound or a longing for care. The dangling paw could represent an exposed, fragile part of the psyche, with the dreamer's empathy reflecting a wish to heal it. The dog becomes a stand-in for the self, needing nurture.

Jungian Interpretation

For Jung, animals often embody instinctual wisdom or archetypes. Reggie could be an anima/animus figure, inner feminine or masculine energy, or a guide from the unconscious, revealing vulnerability as a strength. The injured paw might signal a need to acknowledge emotional wounds as part of individuation.

Gestalt Therapy: Reggie as the Self

In Gestalt terms, Reggie is the dreamer. The paw is a disowned vulnerability, and the dream invites recognition and care. By feeling Reggie's pain, the dreamer begins to integrate this tender part, moving toward wholeness.

Contemporary Insights: Emotional Bonds

Attachment theory might see Reggie as a symbol of secure bonds, with the injury reflecting fears of loss or relational wounds. Neuroscience adds that dreams process empathy, and this dream could strengthen the dreamer's capacity for connection by rehearsing care in a symbolic space.

Contemporary Dream Research: Emotional Regulation and Memory

Beyond Freud and Jung, modern science offers insights into dreaming. Research shows dreams aid emotional regulation and memory consolidation during REM sleep, processing daily experiences into long-term understanding. The gray figure might help grieve, the maze untangle anxiety, and Reggie foster empathy, all as the brain balances emotion.

Studies also suggest dreams act as overnight therapy, confronting fears or unresolved feelings symbolically. This aligns with Freud's tension release and Jung's compensatory balance, grounding their ideas in biology.

What These Dreams Reveal About the Mind

These dreams weave stories our waking minds struggle to tell. They're not random; they're poetic truths. Grief lingers in the gray figure, overwhelm folds into the engulfed train, anxiety loops through the maze, and tenderness shines in Reggie's paw. Freud illuminates desire, Jung archetypes, Gestalt integration, and the science of emotional processing, but the real wisdom is personal.

Your dreams are messages from your psyche, but they are also emotional acts of care. They are your mind trying to help you see, hold, and heal the parts of yourself that are waiting in the dark.

You don't need to be an expert in Freud or Jung to understand your dreams. You just need to be willing to sit with them. To feel them. To ask what they want you to know. Often, they are saying: *This is what still lives in you. This is what needs care.*

In the next chapter, we'll leave behind symbolic interpretation and enter the world of scientific research. How do modern neuroscientists, psychologists, and sleep researchers understand what happens in the brain during dreaming? What role do dreams play in learning, memory, and emotional regulation? If this chapter spoke to the emotional language of dreams, the next one will explore the biology behind the mystery.

12

SCIENTIFIC RESEARCH ON DREAMS

Dreams have long inspired poetry and prophecy, but today they're capturing the attention of neuroscientists, psychologists, and technologists determined to decode what the mind is really doing during sleep. In cutting-edge labs, researchers are going far beyond REM-cycle charts and sleep-stage models. They're using neuroimaging, machine learning, and direct brain-to-dreamer communication to explore dreams as complex cognitive events: emotional processors, memory sculptors, even rehearsal spaces for survival and creativity.

Earlier in this book, I shared the story of a smoky, silent presence that appeared above me just days after my brother died. It wasn't just a vision but a rupture in my understanding of what a dream could be. Today, I wonder what a neuroscientist would see in that moment: Was it a flash of memory encoded in visual cortex patterns? Was my amygdala firing through the fog of grief, generating imagery to help me make sense of loss? Or was my brain trying to integrate emotional trauma into a narrative I could survive?

This chapter doesn't aim to strip dreams of meaning; it's here to expand them. We'll explore how researchers are mapping the neural signatures of specific dream content, using AI to reconstruct images from brain activity, and even communicating with lucid dreamers while they sleep. You'll meet scientists who believe dreams are predictive simulators, emotional regulators, and creative engines, tools the brain uses not just to *cope*, but to *evolve*.

Let's enter the lab, not to explain away the mystery, but to illuminate just how astonishingly intelligent your dreaming mind really is.

DREAM ENCODING AND EMOTIONAL TAGGING: HOW THE BRAIN SORTS WHAT MATTERS

Neuroscience is beginning to confirm what dreamers have long intuited: dreams don't just reflect our memories, they help us *shape* them. During sleep, especially in the deeper phases, the brain becomes an editor, curator, and emotional translator. Researchers studying memory consolidation have found that our brains don't treat all experiences equally. Instead, they prioritize the moments that carry emotional charge: joy, fear, grief, and desire. The brain flags these events through a process known as **emotional tagging**, a kind of neurological highlighting system largely directed by the amygdala, our internal danger, and meaning, detector.

Once a memory is emotionally tagged, it moves through a kind of neurological pipeline. The *hippocampus*, a seahorse-shaped structure deep in the brain that acts like short-term storage for new memories, begins to replay fragments of your recent experience. These fragments don't just sit there; they're gradually passed along to the *neocortex*, the brain's outer layer responsible for higher-order thinking, where they're woven into long-term memory. This transfer process, known as *hippocampal-neocortical dialogu*e, often happens while we sleep, especially in dreams. But it's not a perfect copy-and-paste. It's more like a remix: dreams take the raw material of lived experience, blend it with older memories, and add emotion-driven color to make meaning.

That smoky figure I saw drifting across the ceiling as a child, right after my brother died, may never be something science can fully dissect. But I can now imagine what my brain might have been doing. The intensity of loss was too much to process consciously. My amygdala was likely on high alert, flagging everything with a red warning label: danger, pain, confusion. That image, soft, silent, haunting, could have been my brain's attempt to encode that loss, to find a shape for the unspeakable, and to deposit it gently into long-term memory without fracturing me entirely. It was my mind's way of saying, *"Remember this. It matters. But survive it, too."*

Recent studies by researchers like Matthew Walker and Robert Stickgold support this idea. Their work shows that during sleep, especially in the hours following trauma, the brain processes difficult experiences in a dream state, often removing the emotional sting while preserving the narrative. This explains why we can wake from an intense dream about a painful event and feel just a little more at peace, even if we can't explain why. Dreams may be our emotional archivists, helping us store what hurts in a way that doesn't break us.

In this light, dreams aren't just personal; they're neurological. They're the brain's attempt to help us carry the weight of living.

DREAMS AS EMOTIONAL HEALERS: EASING THE HEART'S BURDENS

One of the most powerful and deeply human discoveries in modern dream research is this: dreams help us metabolize emotion. Not just process it intellectually, but *feel it differently*, more safely, more gently. When we sleep, the brain doesn't simply go offline. Instead, it creates a theater where unresolved feelings can be softened, reframed, and emotionally rehearsed without real-world consequences.

A 2024 study published in *Scientific Reports* revealed something remarkable: people who remembered their dreams were measurably better at handling emotional memories. In the study, participants were shown disturbing images before sleep, and again the next day. Those who recalled dreaming retained the memory content, but without the same emotional sting. It was as if the dreaming brain had "digested" the emotional charge, leaving the story intact but reducing its weight. This supports what many trauma-informed therapists have long suspected: that dreams are the brain's built-in emotional regulation system.

I think back to that night after my brother's death, when I saw the smoky shape drift across my ceiling. I woke not in panic, but with a strange, gentle lightness, like some unspoken sorrow had lifted just enough to let me breathe again. At the time, I had no language for it. Now, science gives me a framework: perhaps my dream had allowed my brain to hold grief without breaking under its weight, to begin integrating it without collapsing into overwhelm.

More recent research from 2023 supports this function even further. Dreaming about stressful experiences, such as arguments, mistakes, or past trauma, can actually reduce anxiety the next day. These dreams act as internal "rehearsals," offering the body and brain a chance to feel difficult emotions in a symbolic or altered context, one that's safer and more contained. It's like emotional exposure therapy conducted by your own subconscious, with no judgment, no risk, and no real-world consequence.

For trauma survivors, this is more than comforting; it's empowering. Studies now suggest that recurring dreams involving painful past events can, over time, help rewire the emotional associations attached to those memories. The brain doesn't erase the past, but it reshapes how we *feel* about it. This makes dreams powerful allies in post-traumatic growth, providing an intuitive and organic path to healing that happens even when we're not consciously trying.

I've noticed that in my own life, too. Whenever I feel overwhelmed or emotionally flooded, I'll sometimes dream of a golden river winding through a quiet forest, always the same light and bend in the path. It's a dream that offers no answers, just peace. And when I wake, something has shifted. Neuroscience tells me why: Dreams may help rebalance brain chemistry and restore emotional equilibrium. But to me, it feels like a soul-level exhale, as if the dream itself is whispering, *"Keep going. You're not alone."*

Far from being meaningless or random, our dreams may be among our brains' most intimate tools to help us survive loss, regulate fear, and rekindle hope.

WHEN DREAMS CARRY TRAUMA: NIGHTMARES, PTSD, AND THE BRAIN'S CRY FOR HEALING

Not all dreams are peaceful. For trauma survivors, dreams often become battlegrounds, haunted by flashbacks, distorted memories, or overwhelming sensations that return night after night. These are not random images. From a neurological perspective, nightmares are the brain's desperate attempt to process what it couldn't resolve while awake.

In individuals with PTSD, the amygdala, the brain's fear center, often remains overactive, even during sleep. At the same time, the prefrontal cortex, which usually helps us interpret and regulate emotions, shows reduced activity. The result? Emotionally intense dreams without the calming voice of reason. That's why trauma dreams can feel so raw and terrifying: the brain is reliving emotion without context, trying again and again to make sense of what happened.

But here's where hope begins to rise. Researchers at Harvard and Stanford have found that trauma-related nightmares may actually serve a therapeutic function if they're allowed to evolve. This evolution can happen through time, therapy, or conscious engagement with the dream. When a trauma dream begins to shift, perhaps the attacker is no longer chasing you, or you find a door where there wasn't one before, it often signals that the brain is beginning to *re-integrate* the traumatic memory with new meaning. Some researchers call this "resolution dreaming," where the subconscious rehearses new, safer outcomes until the emotional charge is reduced.

Neuroscientist Rosalind Cartwright, one of the pioneers of dream research, referred to dreaming as "overnight therapy." Her studies found that people who had recurring dreams of a stressful event, *but who noticed those dreams changing over time*, were more likely to recover from depression and PTSD symptoms. In other words, it's not just that you dream about trauma; it's how your dream *changes* that marks healing.

I've noticed this in myself. In the early months after a painful breakup, I'd dream repeatedly of trying to dial a number that never connected. Always the same panic. Always the same static. But one night, I heard a voice on the line. Just a few words. I woke up crying, but relieved. I hadn't realized how deeply that loss was etched into my nervous system until the dream began to shift. That was my first clue that my body and brain were beginning to let go.

For some, trauma dreams stop altogether. For others, they soften, take on symbolic meaning, or transform into something creative or spiritual. Therapies like *Image Rehearsal Therapy (IRT)* now teach people to rewrite recurring nightmares, rehearsing new outcomes while awake consciously. And research shows this can literally rewire neural pathways, easing fear responses and restoring emotional balance.

So if you find yourself revisiting a nightmare again and again, try this: instead of asking, *"Why is this happening to me?"*, try *"What is my brain trying to resolve?"* You may discover that the dream is not a punishment, but a process; one that's working, quietly and powerfully, to set you free.

DECODING DREAMS WITH AI: SEEING THE INVISIBLE

For most of human history, dreams have lived in mystery: fleeting, fragile, and impossible to fully capture. We wake, remember a few images, maybe write them down, and the rest fades into the ether. But what if we could *see* our dreams? Not just remember them, but reconstruct them: frame by frame, thought by thought? What once belonged to mystics and poets is now entering the realm of data scientists and neural engineers.

In recent years, researchers in Japan, the U.S., and Europe have begun using artificial intelligence to literally *decode visual dreams from the brain*. At institutions like Kyoto University and UC Berkeley, participants are placed in **fMRI** (functional Magnetic Resonance Imaging) scanners while sleeping. These machines track blood flow and activity across specific regions of the brain, especially the visual cortex, where we "see" in both waking and dreaming states. Using machine learning algorithms, researchers then compare the dreamer's brain activity to massive image databases to reconstruct what the person might have seen in their dream.

The results? Crude but stunning. In some studies, AI-generated images matched key elements of the dreams: shapes, objects, even rough landscapes. It's not perfect yet, but the implication is clear: we are inching toward the possibility of externalizing the internal world of dreams.

What excites scientists most isn't just the visual reconstruction: it's what it could mean for understanding the emotional and symbolic content of dreams. Could AI one day help therapists interpret recurring nightmares or uncover buried trauma? Could it become a tool for creative artists to pull imagery directly from the subconscious? Already, AI is being trained to identify emotional tone and symbolic structures in dream journals, helping researchers find patterns too subtle or complex for the human eye alone.

And while that might sound invasive or even dystopian to some, others see it as an act of deep witnessing: a chance to honor the intelligence of the dreaming brain by finally giving it form. One researcher called it "the closest thing we've ever had to dreaming out loud."

For me, it brings back the golden river I so often dream of, a winding light that flows without end. What if one day, I could see that river drawn on a screen, or hold its image in my hands? Would it feel less magical, or more real?

AI may never fully capture the sacred, surreal quality of dreaming. But what it *can* do is help us listen more closely to what our subconscious is already trying to say. In that sense, it's not replacing intuition: it's partnering with it, making the invisible just a little more visible.

Chapter Summary: The Science Behind the Dream

As we've seen, science is catching up to what dreamers have always known deep down, our dreams are intelligent, emotionally charged, and profoundly purposeful. Whether shaped by ancient survival instincts, emotional integration, or neural algorithms, dreams continue to guide, warn, and reveal. And now, with the help of AI and neuroimaging, we're beginning to glimpse the invisible, mapping the private landscapes of the subconscious like never before.

But even as research pushes into high-tech territory, something timeless remains: our need to share what we dream. Across cultures and centuries, people have sat together, around fires, in temples, on couches, and spoken their dreams aloud. Not for scientific validation, but for connection. To be witnessed. To ask, "What do you see in this?" and receive a reflection we couldn't find on our own.

Because while the brain may be the dream's architect, meaning is often built together.

Through the lens of science, we've journeyed deep into the world of dreams, unraveling the mysteries of neuroscience, the innovations of AI, and the intricate ways our emotions are processed as we sleep. These discoveries illuminate the mechanics of dreaming, revealing how our brains weave narratives from the threads of memory, feeling, and imagination. Dreams are not just personal creations of the mind; they are experiences meant to be shared. While science helps us understand the how, it's in sharing our dreams that we begin to grasp the why, finding meaning, connection, and insight in the stories we tell. In the next chapter, we'll explore how communal dream-sharing not only deepens our understanding but also binds us together, transforming the private act of dreaming into a collective adventure.

13

SHARING DREAMS AND GROUP INTERPRETATION

Dreams don't just live in our heads—they come alive when spoken.

For centuries, people have gathered in circles to share dreams. From Indigenous dream lodges to ancient Greek dream temples, from African storytelling to Jungian salons in modern psychotherapy, dream-sharing has always been a communal act—a way of giving meaning to the mysterious and personal through the wisdom of others. When one person speaks their dream aloud, something opens. The dream becomes more than a private image—it becomes a mirror, a message, a conversation.

And we still crave that today. In recent years, online dream-sharing communities have begun to flourish, from Zoom-based dream groups to apps that let you journal and interpret dreams with others. People who've never met in person sit in digital circles, offering reflections, symbolism, and insights, often more thoughtful and tender than the dreamer expected. Whether you're part of a therapist-led group or an informal circle of dreamers, the act of being witnessed changes everything. It's not about getting the "right" interpretation. It's about feeling seen.

HOW CULTURES THROUGHOUT HISTORY APPROACHED COMMUNAL DREAM-SHARING

Long before therapists, group chats, or dream dictionaries, humans were gathering to speak their dreams aloud. In ancient cultures, dreams weren't considered random or private, they were seen as messages from the divine, glimpses into the soul, or guidance for the entire community. And perhaps most importantly, dreams weren't meant to be kept to yourself. They were meant to be shared.

In Indigenous cultures across North America, morning dream-sharing circles were a vital part of daily life. Among the Iroquois and Ojibwe, for example, dreams were treated as instructions from the spirit world. People would rise, gather, and speak their dreams aloud to family or tribal elders. The interpretations weren't just personal, they were communal. A dream about a storm, a lost animal, or a bright light might mean something for the whole village, not just the individual. These dreams guided decisions, healed relationships, and sometimes even predicted danger.

In ancient Egypt, dreams were thought to be a form of divine communication. Egyptians kept detailed dream journals and visited temple priests who specialized in dream interpretation. Dream books were passed down like sacred texts, offering lists of symbols and their meanings. But even then, interpretation was rarely done alone; it happened in community, within spiritual circles, or under the guidance of mentors who knew how to listen for deeper truths.

The Greeks took it even further. In the temples of Asclepius, the god of healing, people would undergo **incubation rituals**, sleeping overnight in temple chambers in hopes of receiving a healing dream. In the morning, they would share what they dreamed with priest-interpreters, who believed that gods spoke through these night visions. Dreams weren't just therapeutic, they were sacred medicine.

In many African traditions, dreams continue to be seen as ancestral communication. Elders, shamans, or diviners often serve as the dream interpreters, helping others understand what their dreams mean for family, tribe, or spiritual growth. It's not unusual for an African village to respond communally to a powerful dream, whether it signals a celebration, a warning, or a calling.

Even in the early Christian and Islamic worlds, dreams were taken seriously and interpreted in the spiritual community. In medieval monasteries, monks recorded their dreams as part of their spiritual growth. And in Islamic tradition, dream interpretation (known as *ta'bir*) is still practiced with reverence, rooted in the belief that dreams can hold divine truths.

All these traditions share this: dreams were never meant to be isolated experiences. They were portals, opened in the dark but brought into the light *together*. And while our modern world has grown quieter about dreams, the longing remains. Many people feel an intuitive pull to share their dreams, but don't always know where or how. That's what the next part of this chapter is here to explore.

THEN AND NOW: HOW MODERN DREAM CIRCLES ECHO ANCIENT WISDOM

Although many of us no longer wake up in huts, temples, or monasteries, the desire to share our dreams and appear in them persists. In fact, more and more people are finding their way back to this ancient practice, using modern tools to create sacred space in new ways.

Instead of gathering around a fire, we gather on Zoom. Instead of temple priests, we find trusted facilitators, therapists, or simply fellow dreamers willing to listen with care. But the essence is the same: we tell our dreams aloud, and others reflect what they see, not to claim authority, but to offer perspective, insight, and resonance. Sometimes, someone else hears the one thing we missed. Sometimes, they simply witness our story and say, *"That matters."*

Modern dream groups are popping up in therapists' offices, spiritual communities, support groups, and even group chats. Some are structured like traditional circles, with guidelines and a shared format. Others are informal, just a few friends texting each other their dreams each morning. And thanks to platforms like Zoom, people from across the globe can now sit "together" and reflect on dreams that feel just as ancient, personal, and mysterious as ever.

Apps like DreamWell or Dreambook offer online journaling tools with the option to share dreams anonymously or in small groups. Websites like IASD (International Association for the Study of Dreams) host online dream salons and educational forums. In Facebook groups, Reddit threads, and private communities, people are reviving the communal dream, not just for interpretation, but for connection.

What's beautiful is that you don't need to be a scholar, therapist, or shaman to take part. All you need is a willingness to listen deeply, share gently, and trust that something meaningful happens when we speak the language of dreams out loud.

In the next section, we'll walk through how to create your own dream-sharing circle—whether you meet on couches or computer screens, and how to keep that space supportive, reflective, and sacred.

HOW TO START YOUR OWN DREAM CIRCLE (ONLINE OR IN-PERSON)

You don't need a psychology degree or a background in spirituality to create a dream circle. All you need is curiosity, a willingness to listen deeply, and a few other dreamers willing to show up with openness and heart. Whether you gather in a living room, on a back porch, or in a Zoom window, dream-sharing becomes a modern return to an ancient practice, a sacred space where our inner worlds are spoken, witnessed, and held.

Gathering the Group

Start with a small group, between three and six people is ideal. These can be close friends, family members, creative peers, or people you meet through online wellness or dream forums. The key isn't expertise; it's emotional safety. A dream circle thrives on mutual respect and shared presence, not on having "the right answers."

Some people begin with an invitation as simple as:

"Would you be interested in meeting regularly to share dreams and reflect on them together?"

You may be surprised how many people are longing for exactly that kind of connection.

Setting the Space

Whether you're meeting in person or online, setting the tone matters. In a physical space, light a candle, arrange cushions, make tea, or play soft music to ground the group. If you're online, invite each participant to bring a comforting item: a warm drink, a journal, or even a candle to light on their screen. These small acts create intentional space and shift everyone gently into the dream-sharing mindset.

Begin each gathering with a short grounding practice—perhaps three deep breaths together, a moment of silence, or a spoken intention, such as:

"We're entering this space with curiosity, compassion, and care. Dreams are gifts, and we treat them with respect."

Choosing a Format

There's no single "right" way to run a dream circle, but here are two simple and effective formats that work beautifully for beginners:

The Deep Listening Circle

1. One person shares a dream in full, without interruption.
2. The group takes turns offering reflections, using the phrase: *"If it were my dream..."* This invites insight without imposing meaning.
3. The dreamer listens without needing to respond or explain.
4. After all reflections, the dreamer may share what resonated or what the dream now feels like.

The Dream Round Format

1. Each participant briefly shares a recent or meaningful dream (1–2 minutes).
2. The group chooses one dream to explore more deeply, using the "If it were my dream…" reflection method.
3. Time permitting, the group may return to shared symbols, patterns, or emotions that echoed across everyone's dreams.

Creating Ground Rules

To keep the space sacred and psychologically safe, agree as a group on a few basic principles:

- **Confidentiality**: What is shared in the circle stays in the circle.
- **Non-judgment**: No dream is too strange, too small, or too heavy.
- **Respect**: We don't analyze the dreamer, we reflect on our own responses.
- **Presence**: Everyone agrees to be fully present and listen with care.

You may choose to read these aloud at the start of each session or revisit them periodically as the group evolves.

Establishing a Rhythm

Consistency helps dreams deepen over time. Consider starting with a simple schedule:

- Weekly or biweekly for 60–90 minutes
- Monthly for longer, more reflective sessions (90–120 minutes)

The key is to create rhythm without pressure. Some weeks will feel rich, others quieter. That's okay. The practice itself is what matters.

To keep things light and meaningful, you can end each session with a short ritual:

- Everyone names one image or feeling they're taking with them.
- A collective journal entry (shared Google Doc or email thread)
- A closing phrase like, *"We honor the dream and the dreamer."*

Note: Consider creating a shared dream journal or group thread where participants can jot down dreams, symbols, or questions between meetings. Over time, you may notice synchronicities, repeating motifs, or overlapping images, a gentle reminder that we're dreaming with each other, not just for ourselves, but in some mysterious way.

FACILITATING DREAM SHARING AND GROUP INTERPRETATION

Dream sharing and group interpretation can unlock profound insights and build meaningful connections among participants. However, these discussions require careful facilitation to ensure they remain productive, respectful, and supportive. This section offers practical strategies for running a dream-sharing group, including how to manage group dynamics, resolve conflicts, and handle emotional moments, along with specific techniques to guide the process effectively.

The Role of the Facilitator

The facilitator's main job is to create a safe, welcoming environment where everyone feels comfortable sharing their dreams. Key responsibilities include:

- Setting and enforcing clear ground rules.
- Encouraging all members to participate equally.
- Keeping the discussion on track and managing time.
- Responding to conflicts or emotional reactions with care.

You don't need to be a dream interpretation expert to facilitate; your role is to guide the process, not to dictate meanings. The dreamer's own insights should always take center stage.

Setting Ground Rules

Clear ground rules help establish a respectful and trusting atmosphere. Before starting, agree on guidelines such as:

- **Confidentiality**: What's shared in the group stays in the group.
- **Respect**: Listen without interrupting and value all perspectives.
- **Focus on the Dreamer**: Ask questions to explore the dream rather than imposing your own interpretation.
- **Voluntary Participation**: No one has to share if they're not ready—passing is always an option.
- **No Advice**: Share personal reflections instead of telling others what to do.

Managing Group Dynamics

Groups naturally include a mix of personalities—some talkative, others reserved. To keep the discussion balanced, try these strategies:

- Use a timer to give each dreamer equal sharing time.
- Gently invite quieter members to contribute by asking, "What are your thoughts on this?"
- If someone dominates, interrupt politely: "Thanks for that, let's hear from someone else now."
- Consider a talking stick or similar tool to take turns speaking.

Handling Emotional Reactions

Dreams can stir up strong feelings, and sharing them might leave someone vulnerable. If a dreamer gets upset:

- Acknowledge their emotions: "It sounds like this dream really touched you."
- Offer a brief pause or break if needed.
- Encourage the group to respond with empathy, perhaps by sharing similar experiences or simply listening.
- Reassure everyone that it's okay to feel emotional in this safe space.

Facilitation Techniques

Good facilitation helps dreamers explore their dreams without feeling judged or directed. Here are some techniques:

- **Open-Ended Questions**:
    - "What stood out most to you in this dream?"
    - "How did you feel when that happened?"
    - "Does anything in your life right now connect to this?"
- **Tentative Interpretations**: Offer ideas lightly to spark reflection, not to define:
    - "I wonder if this could tie into that change you mentioned…"
    - "Could this image point to something you're wrestling with?"
- **Reflective Listening**: Restate what you hear to show understanding:
    - "It seems like you felt trapped in that moment—did I get that right?"

Addressing Common Challenges

Even with the best preparation, issues can pop up. Here's how to handle them:

- **Disagreements Over Meaning**: If interpretations clash, say, "Dreams can mean different things to different people; let's focus on what it means to the dreamer."
- **Dominant Voices**: Redirect gently: "Great input; let's open it up to others now."
- **Sensitive Dreams**: If a dream is intense or personal, ensure the group responds kindly and doesn't push for details.
- **Reluctant Sharers**: Let them know it's fine to listen or ask questions instead.

Conclusion

Facilitating a dream-sharing group takes practice, but with these tools, you can create a space where everyone feels heard and valued. The goal isn't to crack a dream's code; it's to explore it together, respecting each person's unique perspective. Start small, perhaps with a close friend or two, and let the process evolve as you go.

THE DREAM THAT CONNECTS US ALL

Dreams are like whispers from a shared human soul. When we speak them aloud, whether in ancient temples or today's virtual circles, they transform from private tales into bridges, binding us to one another. They become mirrors reflecting our fears and hopes, messages revealing hidden truths, and threads weaving a tapestry of connection. Dreams speak a universal dialect across time, culture, and language, reminding us we're never alone in our inner worlds.

In the hush of a listening circle, dreams ripple beyond the dreamer, sparking empathy and wonder. They challenge us to unravel their meanings and become better dreamers and listeners for ourselves, each other, and the world.

In this chapter, we've explored how sharing dreams among trusted companions reshapes us. It unlocks deeper self-awareness, reveals shared symbols, and forges bonds that transcend the solitary. Dreams, we've discovered, are not just ours alone; they're a collective language of reflection and meaning. And if this practice can transform us, think of its power for the youngest among us. Imagine igniting this spark in children. What if we taught them to embrace their dreams before doubt or fear could dim them? What if nightmares became invitations to courage and curiosity rather than shadows to flee?

14

DREAM EXPLORATION FOR CHILDREN

WHY CHILDREN DREAM DIFFERENTLY

Children don't just dream like adults, they dream *differently*. Their inner world is vivid, unfiltered, and emotionally raw. While an adult dream might bury the truth beneath layers of metaphor and logic, a child's dream often comes rushing in with the force of a flood: direct, intense, and impossible to ignore.

This isn't just poetic; it's neurological. The dreaming brain of a child is still developing. Their emotional regulation systems, memory networks, and cognitive filters are still under construction. That means their dreams are often less restrained by logic and more saturated with feeling. Their subconscious is wide open, and their nervous systems are still learning what safety even *feels* like. So when a child dreams, they're not just processing the day; they're shaping their identity, their emotional range, and their sense of what's real.

I remember one dream from childhood that still sits in my bones: I was caught in raging water, being pulled toward the edge of a massive waterfall. The sound was deafening. My body couldn't fight the current, and I knew, absolutely knew, that I was going to fall. Just before I went over the edge, I woke up, heart pounding, breath caught in my throat. That dream came back again and again, not because I'd actually fallen into water, but because *something* in my young life, grief, fear, powerlessness, was pulling me under. My body remembered what my conscious mind couldn't fully explain.

For many children, dreams feel that big. That uncontrollable. And without the words or context to understand them, these dreams can leave kids confused, afraid, or shut down. That's why how we respond matters so deeply. When we dismiss a child's dream as "just a dream," we teach them not to trust their inner experience. But when we listen, validate, and stay curious, we show them that their feelings are real and that their dreams are a bridge to understanding, not something to run from.

Children also dream more frequently in rich, symbolic narratives, because play and imagination *are* their natural language. What might seem bizarre or nonsensical to us is often loaded with meaning for them. A dream of flying may not just be fun, but also about freedom from school stress or separation anxiety. A monster in the closet might be a stand-in for a bully, a parental argument, or an overwhelming change.

When we take children's dreams seriously, not by over-analyzing, but by staying present and open, we help them learn something invaluable: *their inner world is worth listening to.* And that lesson will carry into every stage of their life.

HOW TO HELP A CHILD RECALL AND SHARE DREAMS

Children's dreams live close to the surface: bright, emotional, and often unfiltered. But they can also slip away quickly, like mist burned off by the sun. A child might wake up from a vivid dream only to forget it by the time they're brushing their teeth. Or they might hold onto it quietly, unsure whether it's something they're allowed to talk about.

Helping a child remember and share their dreams doesn't require special training, just presence, curiosity, and care. It's not about analysis or decoding; it's about building a bridge between their dream world and their waking life, one gentle step at a time.

Start by shaping your home environment to welcome dreams. Both bedtime and morning routines can become soft invitations into this hidden part of your child's inner life.

In the Morning: Keep it Slow and Open-Ended

Mornings are the best time for dream recall, especially before screens, noise, or routine distractions begin. Sit beside your child, make eye contact, and ask with curiosity, not pressure:

- *"Did you dream about anything last night?"*
- *"Did your mind go on any adventures while you were asleep?"*
- *"Was there a color, a person, or a feeling that stayed with you?"*

If they say "no" or "I forget," that's okay. You're not looking for a performance, you're planting the idea that dreams matter and can be shared when they're ready.

At Bedtime: Set the Stage for Dream Invitation

The way we talk about sleep shapes how children enter it. Try making dreams part of the bedtime rhythm—not as something scary or mysterious, but something playful and natural.

- *"I wonder what kind of dream stories will visit you tonight."*
- *"If you could dream anything, what would it be?"*
- *"Let's leave your dream journal nearby, just in case something magical happens."*

This gives the brain a soft cue that dreaming is safe, creative, and welcome.

Create a Dream Journal—Or a Dream Box

Children love rituals and tools. Give them their own dream journal, notebook, or even a "dream box" where they can place drawings, notes, or symbols from their dreams. Let them personalize it however they like.

Here are a few child-friendly options:

- Let them draw scenes or characters from their dream
- Use stickers, colors, or shapes to describe how the dream *felt*
- Have them tell the dream out loud while you write it down for them

There's no wrong way to capture a dream. The goal is to honor the story, not to perfect the memory.

Respond with Curiosity, Not Correction

When a child shares a dream, they're offering you a glimpse into their inner world. This is sacred. Instead of trying to explain it or make sense of it, simply stay curious.

Ask gently:

- "What happened next?"
- "How did you feel in the dream?"
- "What was your favorite (or scariest) part?"

You might reflect back with phrases like:

- "That sounds like such a big adventure."
- "It's amazing how your brain made that up."
- "Thank you for telling me your dream—it's special to hear it."

This builds emotional safety and encourages deeper self-expression.

Validate All Emotions—Even the Scary Ones

If a child shares a nightmare or difficult dream, avoid saying *"It wasn't real."* That may feel dismissive. Instead, help them feel safe while staying with their emotional truth.

Try:

- "That must have been really scary. I'm glad you told me."
- "Sometimes our dreams hold big feelings that want to come out."
- "Would it help to draw the dream or make up a new ending together?"

You can even offer small dream rituals for comfort, like placing a toy "protector" by the bed, or imagining a magical shield around their room before sleep.

Helping a child recall and share their dreams is not about getting the story "right." It's about letting them feel seen. It's about meeting them in the space between imagination and emotion, and telling them, with presence and gentleness: *"Your inner world matters."*

And as you listen, you may find your own dreams waking up again. Because when a child shares their dream, they're not just telling a story, they're offering you an invitation to reconnect with your own.

TURNING NIGHTMARES INTO PLAY AND POWER

When a child wakes from a nightmare, they often don't just feel scared; they feel confused, helpless, and alone. Their heart may be racing, their body tense, and their emotions still swirling even after their eyes are open. For adults, it's tempting to say, *"It wasn't real,"* or *"Just go back to sleep."* But for children, the emotional experience of the dream *was* real, and what they need most is safety, not dismissal.

Nightmares are often the brain's way of working through big emotions. And when met with creativity and compassion, they can become powerful opportunities for healing and growth. Instead of shutting them down, we can help children turn fear into understanding through play, storytelling, and ritual.

After a bad dream, sit with your child and simply listen. Offer comfort with your presence, not just your words. If the dream feels too heavy, invite them to draw it. Putting the dream on paper gives it form and gives the child a sense of control. Ask if they'd like to add anything to the picture: a superhero flying in, a door that leads to safety, or a rainbow that appears just in time. Let their imagination reshape the story.

Another gentle option is dream play. With stuffed animals or puppets, you can act out the dream together, then imagine how it could go differently. When a child turns a nightmare into a story they can change, they begin to feel strong again.

Before bedtime, you might create a small ritual to help them feel protected, nothing complex, just meaningful. A stuffed animal who "stands guard," a special bedtime spray they help mix, or even a whispered mantra like, *"My dreams are safe, and I am loved."* Let the child help invent the ritual. That alone makes it powerful.

The goal isn't to eliminate nightmares. It's to help the child feel they are not alone inside them, and to teach them that even the scariest story can be retold with love, safety, and imagination.

Dream Games, Journals, and Bedtime Rituals

Supporting a child's dream life can be playful and light, too. Some families create "dream boxes" with art supplies, stickers, or small objects representing dream symbols. Others keep a shared dream journal by the bedside, where the child can draw or dictate dreams while still sleepy in the morning.

Before sleep, you might ask, *"What kind of dream would you like to have tonight?"* or invite them to imagine a doorway into a dream world of their choosing. These simple bedtime prompts turn sleep into something curious, not scary.

The key is consistency, not perfection. Whether you write, draw, play, or simply talk, the message to your child is this: *Your dreams matter. I'm here to listen.*

And when children feel safe in their inner world, they begin to trust not just their dreams, but themselves.

THE HEALING POWER OF BEING HEARD

When a child shares a dream, especially a scary or confusing one, they're not just telling you a story. They're handing you a key to their inner world. They're asking, in their own quiet way, *"Can you still see me here?"* And when you respond with gentleness, presence, and curiosity, you give them something that goes far beyond interpretation. You give them the gift of being heard.

That simple act of listening, without judgment, without rushing to explain, is healing. It teaches children (and reminds us) that our emotions, images, and imaginations are worth honoring. That the things we dream, no matter how strange or wild, are clues to what matters most inside us.

Children are natural dreamers, but many adults forget how to dream or take their dreams seriously. By helping a child explore their dreams, you may find your own dream life reawakening. And from that shared space, healing can ripple outward: between parent and child, between past and present, between fear and love.

Beyond Interpretation: Your Dream Journey Continues

In this final chapter, we'll step past the basics and explore what's out there for your ongoing dream journey. I've rounded up resources, practices, and ideas not fully covered earlier, tools, and paths to deepen your connection with dreams. You'll find ways to keep questioning, discovering, and uncovering what your dreams might still hold.

Your journey doesn't end with interpretation. It grows. It shifts. It keeps going.

15

THE JOURNEY BEYOND

Many readers stop at interpretation, but dreams invite so much more. If you feel curious, pulled, or even restless by what hasn't yet been explored in this book, here are some powerful directions to continue your dream journey:

DREAMS AND ANCESTRAL MEMORY – LISTENING TO WHAT CAME BEFORE

Some dreams may not belong only to you. Across time and culture, many people have reported dreams that seem to echo lives, stories, or memories they never consciously lived. These are the dreams of ancestral memory, where the psyche becomes a vessel for inherited emotion, resilience, and unfinished legacy.

Take Thomas, for example. He'd never been to the Appalachian mountains, yet he kept dreaming of a weathered log cabin tucked in a foggy forest, always arriving just as an old man; his "grandfather," though not someone he recognized, was sharpening tools by a hearth. Each dream was quiet but saturated with emotion, and Thomas often woke with the scent of smoke lingering in his mind. One night, the dream shifted. The man handed him a carved walking stick and said,

"You have work to do." Thomas later learned, through family research, that his great-grandfather had lived in those exact mountains and was a healer known for carving staffs.

Dreams like these may not always come with such clarity, but they often leave a feeling: "This is not just mine." You might dream of a war-torn village and wake with sorrow you cannot place. You might see faces you've never met but somehow miss. These dream residues may be what Jung called the collective unconscious or cultural and familial memories passed down epigenetically or psychically through our bloodlines.

In Indigenous cultures worldwide, dreaming is not a private act: it's a communal, ancestral one. The Temiar people of Malaysia engage in "dream sharing" each morning to discern ancestral messages. In parts of West Africa, dreams are seen as dialogues with the spirit realm—ancestors, guardians, and elders offering wisdom. Even in modern therapeutic practices, ancestral dreamwork has found its way into modalities like Family Constellations, where unresolved familial trauma is believed to be carried across generations.

If you're curious about your own ancestral dreams, consider asking:

- Do I ever dream of places, people, or time periods I've never known but feel strangely drawn to?
- Do certain family names, heirlooms, or traditions show up in my dreams?
- What emotional themes—abandonment, strength, silence, survival—seem to echo through my lineage?

Journaling Prompt:

Write a dream where you felt connected to something older than yourself. Then ask: *Is this mine, or did I inherit it? What might this dream want healed?*

Guided Meditation Suggestion:

Before bed, place a photo or item from your family lineage near your bedside. Light a candle or say a quiet intention: *"May my dreams show me what my ancestors wish to pass on or let go."* Upon waking, write freely without editing. What came through might not be linear but trust the symbols.

Dreams can be the meeting ground between your modern life and ancient memory. They ask us not just to look forward, but to also look back, gently, reverently, and with curiosity.

And when we listen? Sometimes the past finds peace.

ENERGY, CHAKRAS, AND THE SUBTLE BODY IN DREAMS – THE BODY BEYOND THE BODY

If you've ever felt a dream not just in your mind, but in your chest, gut, or along your spine, then you've already brushed against the energetic dimension of dreaming. Dreams don't just speak in symbols—they pulse, vibrate, burn, or dissolve within the subtle layers of the body.

Across healing traditions, Ayurveda, Traditional Chinese Medicine, and Indigenous energy practices, there's a shared belief that dreams can reflect the health, blockages, or awakenings of the body's unseen systems: the chakras, the meridians, the nadis, or the flow of qi and prana. These systems aren't metaphorical. They are experienced through sensation, intuition, and the body's quiet responses.

Consider Lena, who dreamed of standing in a desert, unable to speak. In the dream, her throat burned. She would try to cry out, but no sound came. When she woke, she felt a pressure at the base of her throat that lingered through the day. After reflecting with a healer, she realized she'd been silencing her truth in waking life, swallowing years of resentment and unsaid words. Her dream pointed to a blocked **throat chakra**, the energetic center of communication.

Others dream of flying and feel a tingling rush along the spine, often linked to **kundalini energy**—the dormant life force said to coil at the base of the spine and rise through the chakras during spiritual growth. Some dream of being pierced in the heart or protected by golden light—sensations that may correspond to the **heart chakra**, where grief and love inter-mingle.

Eastern philosophies are not the only ones that speak this language. In Andean cosmology, dreams are one way to restore *ayni*: sacred reciprocity between the energetic body and the living world. In many Indigenous North American traditions, energy and spirit are not separated, and dreams are felt as "messages through the body," often arising from disharmony or healing that is needed.

When you begin to explore your dreams through the lens of the energetic body, new insights open:

- **Did you feel a part of your body "light up" in a dream?**
- **Were you wounded, embraced, or healed in a particular area?**
- **Did colors, animals, or weather patterns cluster around your chest, belly, hands, or feet?**

These aren't just details—they're invitations.

Journaling Prompt:

Write about a dream where you experienced a strong bodily sensation. Ask yourself: *Where did I feel it? What emotion was attached? Which chakra or body part might this relate to—and what in my waking life echoes that feeling?*

Bedtime Practice:

Place one hand over your heart or belly before sleep. Inhale gently and say silently, *"Show me what I need to feel in my body tonight."* Let your breath guide the dreamwork—not just for insight, but for somatic restoration.

Dreams that speak through the body are often the ones we remember most vividly. They bypass logic and go straight to where we live—in sensation, in emotion, in movement. They remind us that healing isn't only about understanding. Sometimes it's about feeling. And letting your dream guide you—not just through the night, but back into your body.

CREATIVE EXPRESSION THROUGH DREAMS – LET THE DREAM SPEAK AGAIN

Not all dreams are puzzles to be solved. Some are songs waiting to be sung. Images that ache to be painted. Emotions that beg to be danced.

Dreams are one of the purest forms of creative energy. They arrive unfiltered by logic, unshaped by perfectionism. They slip through the cracks of consciousness carrying stories, sensations, and symbols that words alone can't always contain. And when we create from them, not to interpret but to respond, we meet the dream in a different way: not as analysts, but as artists.

Consider Maya, a sculptor who kept dreaming of a house made entirely of feathers. The house would tremble in storms but never collapse. She couldn't explain the dream, so she began to build it—one feather at a time, forming a small clay sculpture covered in soft down she collected over weeks. When she finished, she finally cried. "It's the grief I've carried," she said. "But it didn't fall."

Art gives the dream a second life. Sometimes that life is a poem, other times a melody or a piece of choreography that moves the feeling through the body. Children do this instinctively, turning nightmares into crayon battles or angel stories. Adults often forget. But when we return to this way of knowing—of expressing—we re-enter the magic of the dream without needing to fully understand it.

Let your hands do what your mind can't.

Try this:

- Take one image from a recent dream, a staircase, a bird, a voice, and draw it, no matter your skill.
- Write a free-form poem based on the emotion of a dream, not its storyline.
- Move your body in response to how the dream made you feel. Was it heavy? Flighty? Wild?
- Reimagine the dream's ending. Give it a new chapter.

Creative Journaling Prompt:

What part of the dream wants to be seen, touched, moved, or sung? If it had a color, what would it be? If it had a shape, a texture, a rhythm, what might it become?

Your creative expression doesn't need to be "good." It just needs to be true. The dream already did its job—it visited you. Now you get to visit it back. To respond with curiosity, reverence, or even play. Because in the space between dream and creation, something beautiful happens:

The dream speaks again—this time, through your hands.

DREAMS AND SPIRITUAL GUIDANCE – WHEN THE SOUL SPEAKS

Some dreams don't feel like dreams at all. They arrive differently—calmer, brighter, or charged with a stillness that lingers long after waking. You don't rush to analyze them. You sit with them. You carry them. They feel like *something more.*

These are spiritual dreams—the ones that echo with messages beyond the personal, where time bends, meaning expands, and the dream seems to come *to* you rather than *from* you.

Maybe you've dreamed of someone you lost, and they appeared not as a memory but as a presence—vivid, speaking clearly, leaving you with a peace you hadn't felt in years. Or perhaps you've had a dream that felt like a prophecy; a knowing that came true days or months later. These experiences aren't uncommon. Cultures across the world have revered dreams as sacred communication from the beyond.

In ancient Greece, people sought healing at the temples of Asclepius, where dreams were incubated to receive guidance from the gods. In the Islamic tradition, dreams are seen as one of the 46 parts of prophecy. Many Indigenous traditions believe dreams are bridges between the seen and unseen worlds—a place where spirits, ancestors, and nature speak.

Even in modern times, countless dreamers describe waking from such a dream with tears, clarity, or the unshakable sense that they were being "spoken to." These dreams don't ask to be dissected. They ask to be honored.

If you've ever felt this, you're not imagining it. You're experiencing what Jung called the *numinous*—the presence of something greater than the self, experienced through the symbolic and mysterious language of the dream.

Reflection Practice:

- Recall a dream that stayed with you for weeks or years. What feeling does it hold? Reverence? Comfort? A call to action?
- Was there a figure or symbol that felt otherworldly or sacred?
- Did the dream bring peace, insight, or timing that felt "too perfect" to be a coincidence?

Dream Ritual:

Before bed, you might light a candle or sit quietly with your hand on your heart and whisper an invitation: *"If there is a message meant for me tonight, I'm listening."* Keep a journal nearby. Not to decode, but to witness. Let your dream be what it is—a visitation, a guide, a sacred echo.

Some dreams come to soothe. Some come to awaken. Some come to remind you that you are not walking this life alone.

When a dream touches the soul, it doesn't need to be solved. It only needs to be received.

CONCLUSION

Dear reader,

As we reach the final pages of this book, I want to pause and speak to you, not as an author to an audience, but as one dreamer to another, heart to heart. Writing this has been a journey for me, a chance to sift through the quiet corners of my own mind and soul, and I know that reading it has been a journey for you, too. Together, we've wandered through the landscapes of dreams, their science, their symbols, their mysteries, and I hope you've felt, even for a moment, that you're not alone in the questions they stir.

You've explored so much within these chapters: the way your subconscious whispers truths you might not hear in daylight, the way a nightmare can become a guide if you're brave enough to listen, the way a simple dream journal can unlock doors you didn't know were there. I hope you've come to see your dreams as I've come to see mine, not as fleeting shadows, but as pieces of you, reflections of your deepest self, asking to be noticed.

I want you to know something: your dreams matter. They are not random or trivial. They are your emotions, your memories, your hopes, and sometimes even your healing, all woven into a language that's yours alone. Whether they're wild and vivid or soft and fleeting, they are a gift; a way for your soul to reach out, to process, to grow. And you, simply by being here, by turning these pages and wondering about your own nights, have already begun to honor that gift.

As you close this book, I invite you to keep your dream journal close, to scribble down those morning fragments, even when they feel small or strange. There's no right or wrong way to listen to your dreams, just the way that feels true to you. Maybe you'll share them with someone you trust, or maybe they'll stay your quiet sanctuary. Either way, they're yours to hold, to explore, to learn from.

Thank you for letting me walk beside you through this. It's been a privilege to share my own path and to imagine yours unfolding too. You don't need to have all the answers about your dreams, and you don't need to solve them like puzzles. All they ask is that you keep showing up: curious, open, and willing to hear what they have to say.

So here's my wish for you: May your nights be a gentle bridge to your most authentic self. May your dreams light the way, even when the path feels uncertain. And may you always find the courage to wake up and carry their wisdom into your days.

So keep dreaming.

Keep listening.

And above all, keep waking up.

With gratitude and warmth,

M. Sallie

APPENDIX A: DREAM YOGA – AWAKENING WITHIN THE DREAM

"The dream shows the inner truth and reality of the patient as it really is: not as I conjecture it to be, and not as he would like it to be, but as it is."

— CARL JUNG

The Origins and Lineage of Dream Yoga

"The dream is not just a message. It is a path."

Dream Yoga is a profound and ancient spiritual practice, far from a modern invention, deeply rooted in Tibetan Buddhism. It holds a special place within the Dzogchen and Mahamudra schools, which focus on the direct realization of the mind's true nature, an awakened state of pure awareness beyond ordinary thought. Far more than a technique for lucid dreaming, Dream Yoga transforms the dream state into a sacred training ground for enlightenment, offering practitioners a unique path to explore the illusory nature of reality and prepare for the ultimate transition of death.

Historical Roots in Tibetan Buddhism

The origins of Dream Yoga trace back to the 8th century, with its earliest known written teachings attributed to **Padmasambhava**, the revered Indian tantric master also known as Guru Rinpoche. Padmasambhava played a pivotal role in bringing Buddhism to Tibet, and his teachings laid the foundation for many esoteric practices, including Dream Yoga. However, the practice is likely far older than these written records suggest. Like many spiritual traditions in Tibet, Dream Yoga was initially transmitted orally, passed down from teacher to student through **unbroken lineages** of inner wisdom long before it was documented in texts.

Key texts, such as the *Tantra of the All-Creating King* (a Dzogchen scripture) and the *Six Yogas of Naropa* (a set of advanced practices from the Kagyu lineage), preserve these teachings. Within the *Six Yogas*, Dream Yoga is highlighted as a vital method for attaining enlightenment. These writings emphasize that dreams are not mere subconscious wanderings but powerful reflections of the mind's projections, mirrors of the waking state, equally illusory yet rich with potential for spiritual growth. By mastering the dream state, practitioners can dissolve the boundaries between dreaming and waking life, realizing the **emptiness (shunyata)** of all phenomena.

The Role of Lineage

In Tibetan Buddhism, the authenticity and transformative power of Dream Yoga depend heavily on its **lineage**—the direct transmission of teachings from realized masters to their students. This lineage ensures that the practice remains pure, carrying intellectual knowledge and the experiential insight of enlightenment itself. Legendary figures like **Padmasambhava**, **Naropa**, and **Milarepa** are central to this tradition, each embodying the profound realization that Dream Yoga seeks to cultivate.

The oral nature of this transmission reflects its esoteric character. Dream Yoga was traditionally a closely guarded teaching, shared only with disciples who demonstrated sufficient spiritual maturity. It is often taught alongside other advanced practices, such as *Tummo* (inner heat yoga) and *Phowa* (transference of consciousness), forming part of a holistic path to liberation within the Dzogchen and Mahamudra traditions.

Purpose: A Path to Awakening

Dream Yoga transcends the simple goal of achieving lucidity in dreams, though that is an essential step. Its deeper purpose is to harness the dream state as a tool for **spiritual awakening**. In Tibetan Buddhism, dreams are seen as a "special training ground" because they reveal the mind's creative power more vividly than waking life. By recognizing and working within this state, practitioners gain insight into the nature of reality and prepare for the **bardo**, the intermediate state after death, where similar mental projections arise.

The practice unfolds in stages:

1. **Dream Recall**: Training to vividly remember dreams upon waking.
2. **Lucidity**: Cultivating awareness within the dream, recognizing it as a dream while it occurs.
3. **Transformation**: Manipulating the dream's content—turning fear into peace, for instance—to reflect mastery over mental projections.
4. **Meditation**: Engaging in deep contemplation within the dream, directly experiencing the mind's true nature.

These steps are not just psychological exercises; they carry profound spiritual meaning. Transforming a dream, for example, symbolizes the ability to transcend dualistic thinking, while meditating in a dream offers a direct encounter with the emptiness and interdependence of all things.

Significance and Transformative Power

Dream Yoga's significance lies in its ability to bridge the dream state and waking life, revealing their shared illusory essence. Its benefits are both practical and transcendent:

- **Heightened Awareness**: Lucidity in dreams fosters mindfulness in daily life.
- **Mental Mastery**: Control over dreams reduces attachment to fleeting illusions.
- **Preparation for Death**: By navigating dream projections, practitioners rehearse for the bardo's visions.
- **Realization of Reality**: The practice unveils the mind's role in constructing both dreams and waking experiences, leading to liberation.

In the words of the tradition, "The dream is not just a message. It is a path." Dream Yoga elevates dreaming from a passive experience to an active gateway, guiding practitioners toward a deeper understanding of the mind and the ultimate truth of existence. Rooted in the ancient wisdom of Tibetan Buddhism and carried forward through sacred lineages, it remains one of the world's most esoteric and transformative spiritual practices.

Dream Yoga and the Six Bardos: A Framework for Transformation

Dream Yoga is a profound spiritual practice rooted in Tibetan Buddhism, where it is classified as one of the **Six Bardos**. The term *Bardo* translates to "intermediate state"—a transitional phase between one condition and another, rich with potential for insight and liberation. These Bardos map out the continuum of existence, from waking life to death and beyond, and Dream Yoga occupies a pivotal role within this system.

The Six Bardos Explained

1. **Bardo of This Life (Waking Experience)**
   - This is our everyday state of consciousness—how we perceive the world through our senses, thoughts, and sense of self. It's the starting point for spiritual practice, as our habits and awareness here influence all other Bardos.
2. **Bardo of Meditation**
   - This refers to the state achieved during deep meditation, where the mind becomes calm, focused, and free from distraction. It's a training ground for cultivating the stability and clarity needed for practices like Dream Yoga.
3. **Bardo of Dream** △
   - This is the realm of Dream Yoga. When we dream, our mind constructs an entire reality—people, places, emotions—that feels vivid and real, yet dissolves upon waking. By becoming lucid (aware that you're dreaming) and meditating within this state, you can explore the illusory nature of experience, a skill that extends far beyond sleep.
4. **Bardo of the Moment of Death**
   - This Bardo begins as the body shuts down and consciousness starts to detach from the physical form. It's a critical transition where maintaining awareness can lead to liberation or influence what comes next.
5. **Bardo of the Radiant Light (Dharmata)**
   - After death, the mind encounters a brilliant, pure light—the essence of its own nature. For those unprepared, this moment passes quickly, but practitioners trained in Dream Yoga can recognize and rest in this light, achieving enlightenment.
6. **Bardo of Becoming (Rebirth)**
   - If liberation isn't attained, the mind moves into this Bardo, where karmic tendencies propel it toward a new incarnation. Awareness cultivated through Dream Yoga

can guide this process, potentially leading to a more favorable rebirth or breaking the cycle entirely.

Why the Bardo of Dream Matters

The dream state is no mere curiosity; it's a powerful mirror of the death process. In both dreams and the Bardos of death, the familiar structures of form, ego, and perception dissolve, giving way to fluid, mind-created experiences. If you can wake up within a dream, realizing it's a projection, you can train to do the same during death, recognizing the visions and sensations as illusions rather than realities to cling to. This is why Dream Yoga is often called **"preparation for death."** As a Tibetan proverb puts it: *"If you want to prepare for dying, prepare by waking up in your dreams."*

By mastering lucidity in the Bardo of Dream, practitioners rehearse for the ultimate in-between states, turning sleep into a practice for liberation rather than a break from waking life.

Dream Yoga and Indian Tantric Influence: A Shared Legacy

Dream Yoga didn't emerge on its own; it's deeply connected to **Indian Tantric Yoga**, particularly within **Vajrayana Buddhism**, the tantric branch of Tibetan Buddhism known as the "Diamond Vehicle." This tradition sees the body, energy, and mind as interconnected tools for awakening, and dreams as a subtle layer of consciousness, the *"mind of appearance"*, that can be directly shaped and explored.

Tantric Roots and Practices

Indian tantric traditions, which influenced Tibetan Buddhism starting around the 8th century, emphasize transforming ordinary experiences into paths to enlightenment. Dream Yoga shares this approach, drawing on several related practices:

- **Deity Yoga**: Practitioners visualize themselves as enlightened beings (deities) to embody qualities like compassion or wisdom. In Dream Yoga, this might mean maintaining that

deity identity within a lucid dream, reinforcing the sense that the self is fluid and sacred.
- **Mantra Recitation**: These sacred syllables, chanted aloud or silently, focus the mind and invoke spiritual energy. Reciting a mantra in a lucid dream can deepen concentration and anchor awareness amidst the dream's shifting scenes.
- **Phowa (Consciousness Transference)**: An advanced practice for directing consciousness at death to a pure realm or enlightened state, Phowa relies on the same lucidity and intentionality honed in Dream Yoga.

The Bigger Picture

In Vajrayana, dreams aren't just random—they're opportunities to work with the mind's subtlest layers. By training in the dream state, practitioners uncover the emptiness and luminosity of all phenomena, realizing that waking life, like a dream, is a projection of consciousness. This insight aligns with the tantric goal of seeing the **nature of self, mind, and ultimate reality** as interconnected and beyond grasping.

Dream Yoga vs. Western Lucid Dreaming: Purpose Over Play

At first glance, Dream Yoga and Western lucid dreaming seem similar—both involve becoming aware within a dream. But their intentions and outcomes diverge sharply.

Western Lucid Dreaming

This practice gained prominence in the 1970s through pioneers like Keith Hearne and Stephen LaBerge, who used EEG studies to confirm that lucid dreamers could signal awareness from within sleep. Its appeal lies in:

- **Control**: Shaping the dream to fly, meet idols, or rewrite scenarios.
- **Exploration**: Solving problems or sparking creativity.
- **Creative Play**: Enjoying the dreamscape as a playground.

- **Trauma Healing**: Confronting fears or processing emotions in a safe space.

These are valuable pursuits, often grounded in psychology or personal growth, with scientific backing to prove their reality.

Dream Yoga

Dream Yoga, however, transcends these aims:

- **Liberation**: It's not about controlling the dream but seeing through it. The goal is to realize there's no fixed "dreamer," only pure awareness witnessing the play of mind.
- **Spiritual Depth**: It uses dreams as a meditation space to probe the nature of reality, not just to enjoy or tweak it.
- **Death Preparation**: Lucidity in dreams trains the mind for the Bardos of death, where similar awareness can lead to enlightenment.

The Core Difference

Western lucid dreaming often says, *"You're the dreamer, take charge!"* Dream Yoga counters, *"There is no dreamer—let go of attachment and wake up to awareness."* Tibetan masters like **Tenzin Wangyal Rinpoche, Chögyal Namkhai Norbu,** and **His Holiness the Dalai Lama** emphasize that without a spiritual compass, lucid dreaming risks becoming mere amusement, missing the deeper call to awakening.

Lineage Holders and Teachers: Stewards of Wisdom

Dream Yoga has been handed down through the centuries by enlightened masters who embodied and refined the practice. Here's a closer look at these key figures:

- **Padmasambhava (8th century)**: The legendary founder of Tibetan Buddhism, he brought Dream Yoga from India,

teaching that dreams reflect reality's illusory nature and can lead to liberation.
- **Milarepa (1052–1135)**: Tibet's beloved yogi-poet spent years in cave retreats, using Dream Yoga to deepen his realization amid solitude and hardship.
- **Naropa and Tilopa (10th–11th centuries)**: Indian tantric adepts who shaped the **Six Yogas of Naropa**, including Dream Yoga, influencing Tibetan practices with their radical methods.
- **Chögyal Namkhai Norbu (1938–2018)**: A Dzogchen master who introduced Dream Yoga to the West, favoring natural awareness over forced techniques.
- **Tenzin Wangyal Rinpoche (b. 1961)**: Author of *The Tibetan Yogas of Dream and Sleep*, he bridges ancient wisdom with modern life, making Dream Yoga widely accessible.
- **His Holiness the Dalai Lama (b. 1935)**: The global face of Tibetan Buddhism, he champions Dream Yoga as a tool for meditation, healing, and preparing for death.

These teachers didn't just preserve Dream Yoga—they lived it, adapting it across cultures and eras to guide others toward awakening.

Cultural and Historical Roots

Dream Yoga, a profound spiritual discipline, is deeply rooted in the ancient traditions of Tibetan Buddhism, particularly within the Dzogchen and Mahamudra schools. Far more than a modern invention or a simple technique for lucid dreaming, this time-tested practice traces its origins back to the 8th century, with revered masters like Padmasambhava playing a pivotal role in its development. Yet, its true beginnings likely extend even further into the past, carried through oral traditions by enlightened teachers long before being documented in texts. Understanding these cultural and historical roots is essential, as it situates Dream Yoga within a rich spiritual lineage, lending it authenticity and depth. Rooted in the ancient wisdom of Tibetan

Buddhism, Dream Yoga has been passed down through centuries, offering practitioners a sacred path aimed at enlightenment and a direct connection to the ultimate goal of spiritual awakening.

1. Cultural and Historical Roots

Your summary doesn't yet mention that Dream Yoga is deeply rooted in **Tibetan Buddhism**, particularly within traditions like **Dzogchen** and **Mahamudra**. This context is crucial because it situates Dream Yoga within a rich spiritual lineage, tracing back to ancient masters like **Padmasambhava** in the 8th century, though its oral traditions may be even older.

- **Why it's important**: Highlighting this origin shows that Dream Yoga isn't a modern invention or just about lucid dreaming—it's a time-tested practice aimed at enlightenment, giving it authenticity and depth.

Suggestion: Add a phrase like, "Rooted in the ancient wisdom of Tibetan Buddhism, Dream Yoga has been passed down through centuries by enlightened masters."

2. The Role of Lucidity and Meditation

While you allude to turning sleep into a sacred practice, the specific process of Dream Yoga—becoming lucid and meditating within dreams—could be clarified. It involves:

- Recognizing you're dreaming.
- Maintaining awareness without waking.
- Meditating in the dream to explore the nature of mind.
- **Why it's important**: This structured progression is a hallmark of Dream Yoga, distinguishing it from casual lucid dreaming and underscoring its meditative purpose.

Suggestion: Expand with, "By cultivating lucidity and meditating within dreams, it transforms sleep into a conscious practice of self-discovery."

3. Connection to the Bardos

You mention preparation for death, which is excellent, but explicitly linking Dream Yoga to the **Bardo of Dream** and **Bardo of Death** would strengthen this point. In Tibetan Buddhism, mastering the dream state is a rehearsal for navigating the afterlife with awareness, potentially leading to liberation.

- **Why it's important**: This connection is a core motivation for the practice, making it more than a personal growth tool—it's a spiritual preparation for the ultimate transition.

Suggestion: Enhance with, "It prepares us for the bardos—the transitional states of dream and death—offering a path to liberation."

4. Practical Benefits in Waking Life

Your summary focuses on the spiritual journey, but Dream Yoga also offers tangible benefits for daily living, such as:

- **Enhanced mindfulness** and focus.
- **Emotional healing** through confronting dream scenarios.
- **Creative problem-solving** inspired by the dream state.
- **Why it's important**: Including these makes Dream Yoga relatable and appealing to a broader audience, showing its relevance beyond death preparation.

Suggestion: Add, "It also sharpens mindfulness and heals emotions, enriching our waking lives."

5. The Nature of Reality

Dream Yoga challenges our perceptions by revealing the dreamlike nature of both sleeping and waking states, aligning with the Buddhist concept of **emptiness (shunyata)**—the idea that all phenomena lack inherent existence.

- **Why it's important**: This philosophical depth is a cornerstone of Dream Yoga, making it a profound tool for understanding consciousness and reality itself.

Suggestion: Weave in, "It blurs the line between illusion and truth, revealing the nature of reality as a projection of the mind."

Summary: Sleep as a Sacred Journey

Dream Yoga, rooted in the ancient wisdom of Tibetan Buddhism, is more than a technique; it's a map to the subtle realms, illuminating the spaces between life and death, thought and stillness, illusion and truth. Cultivating lucidity and meditating within dreams transforms sleep into a sacred practice, sharpening mindfulness and healing emotions in waking life while preparing us for the bardo, the transitional states of dream and death. As the Tibetan saying warns, "*If you do not practice Dream Yoga, your sleep is wasted.*" This path offers a rare gift: the chance to turn rest into revelation, blurring the line between illusion and truth to awaken us to a deeper, more conscious way of living and dying.

REFERENCES

The following references have been curated to support a wide-ranging understanding of dream interpretation, lucid dreaming, cultural symbolism, neuroscience, and subconscious exploration.

PositivePsychology.com. "21 mindfulness exercises & activities for adults." Accessed April 1, 2023. https://positivepsychology.com/mindfulness-exercises-techniques-activities

World of Lucid Dreaming. "30 common dream symbols and their meanings." Accessed April 1, 2023. https://www.world-of-lucid-dreaming.com/30-common-dream-symbols.html

Parade. "57 common dreams and their hidden meanings." Accessed April 1, 2023. https://parade.com/health/common-dreams-meanings

Wikipedia. "Activation-synthesis hypothesis." Accessed April 1, 2023. https://en.wikipedia.org/wiki/Activation-synthesis_hypothesis

Ancient Origins. "Asklepion and the use of dreams for curing diseases with help from gods." Accessed April 1, 2023. https://www.ancient-origins.net/ancient-places-europe/asklepion-and-use-dreams-curing-diseases-help-gods-001049

Aunty Flo. "Door dream dictionary: Interpret now!" Accessed April 1, 2023. https://www.auntyflo.com/dream-dictionary/door

Barrett, D. "Dreams and creative problem-solving." Accessed April 1, 2023. https://doi.org/10.1111/nyas.13412

Belanger, E. "Using your dreams for personal growth and healing." Accessed April 1, 2023. https://erikabelanger.com/dreams-kari-hohne

Bible Odyssey. "Prophetic dreams and visions in the Hebrew Bible." Accessed April 1, 2023. https://stock.bibleodyssey.com/articles/prophetic-dreams-and-visions-in-the-hebrew-bible

Calinawan, J. "How to analyze a dream using Jungian dream analysis." Accessed April 1, 2023. https://jonahcalinawan.com/blog/jungian-dream-analysis

Calm. "How to lucid dream: 6 tips to train your body and mind." Accessed April 1, 2023. https://www.calm.com/blog/how-to-lucid-dream

Cartwright, R. D. "The twenty-four hour mind: The role of sleep and dreaming in our emotional lives." Oxford University Press, 2010

CBN. "Guidelines for successfully interpreting spiritual dreams." Accessed April 1, 2023. https://cbn.com/article/holy-spirit/guidelines-successfully-interpreting-spiritual-dreams

Britannica. "Chester Beatty Papyrus." Accessed April 1, 2023. https://www.britannica.com/topic/Chester-Beatty-Papyrus

Wikipedia. "Collective unconscious." Accessed April 1, 2023. https://en.wikipedia.org/wiki/Collective_unconscious

CreativeMindLife. "How to use dream work for personal growth." Accessed April 1,

2023. https://creativemindlife.com/how-to-use-dream-work-for-personal-growth

Dreamly App. "Cultural differences in dream interpretation: A global perspective." Accessed April 1, 2023. https://www.dreamly-app.com/dreams-interpretation-cultural-differences-in-dream-interpretation-a-global-perspective

Domhoff, G. W. (2003). The Scientific Study of Dreams: Neural Networks, Cognitive Development, and Content Analysis. American Psychological Association.

Jung, C. G. (1964). Man and His Symbols. Dell Publishing.

Revonsuo, A. (2000). The reinterpretation of dreams: An evolutionary hypothesis of the function of dreaming. Behavioral and Brain Sciences, 23(6), 877-901.

Walker, M. (2017). Why We Sleep: Unlocking the Power of Sleep and Dreams. Scribner.

Parkway West Pathfinder. "Decoding the depths of dreamscapes." Last modified May 15, 2024. https://pwestpathfinder.com/2024/05/15/decoding-the-depths-of-dreamscapes

KATU. "Developing your intuition through your dreams." Accessed April 1, 2023. https://katu.com/afternoon-live/lifestyle-health/developing-your-intuition-through-your-dreams

GoodTherapy. "Dream analysis: Benefits, techniques & how it works." Accessed April 1, 2023. https://www.goodtherapy.org/learn-about-therapy/types/dream-analysis

Medium. "Dream interpretation: Insights from psychology." Accessed April 1, 2023. https://medium.com/@blog.spot/dream-interpretation-insights-from-psychology-7b678492a978

Dream Moods. "Dream Moods A–Z dream dictionary." Accessed April 1, 2023. https://www.dreammoods.com/dreamdictionary

Dream Moods. "History and background of dreams." Accessed April 1, 2023. http://www.dreammoods.com/dreaminformation/history.htm

Dream Studies. "How to keep a dream journal." Accessed April 1, 2023. https://dreamstudies.org/how-to-keep-a-dream-journal

Little Explainers. "Dream talks: Making sense for kids!" Accessed April 1, 2023. https://www.littleexplainers.com/how-to-explain-dreams-to-a-child

Artsper Blog. "Dreams throughout art." Accessed April 1, 2023. https://blog.artsper.com/en/a-closer-look/dreams-throughout-art

Dream Decoder Dictionary. "Symbolism of dreams in different faiths." Accessed April 1, 2023. https://dict.dreamdecoder.me/symbol/dream-symbolism-different-faiths

Dreamly App. "The impact of dreams on decision-making." Accessed April 1, 2023. https://www.dreamly-app.com/dreams-interpretation-the-impact-of-dreams-on-decision-making-unlocking-the-power-of-the-subconscious-mind

Dreamly App. "Understanding children's dreams: Meanings and interpretations." Accessed April 1, 2023. https://www.dreamly-app.com/dreams-interpretation-understanding-childrens-dreams-meanings-and-interpretations

Emory University. "Lucid dreaming and creativity." Last modified May 3, 2021. https://scholarblogs.emory.edu/artsbrain/2021/05/03/lucid-dreaming-and-creativity

Wikipedia. "Epic of Gilgamesh." Accessed April 1, 2023. https://en.wikipedia.org/wiki/Epic_of_Gilgamesh

Ermshar, A. "The psychology of dreams: Decoding the symbolism and meaning."

Accessed April 1, 2023. https://www.drannetteermshar.com/the-psychology-of-dreams-decoding-the-symbolism-and-meaning

Freud, S. "The interpretation of dreams (Standard Edition, Vols. 4–5)." Hogarth Press, 1900

Harley Therapy. "Freud vs Jung – Similarities and differences." Accessed April 1, 2023. https://www.harleytherapy.co.uk/counselling/freud-vs-jung-similarities-differences.htm

Simply Psychology. "Freud's theory of the unconscious mind." Accessed April 1, 2023. https://www.simplypsychology.org/unconscious-mind.html

Medium. "Mapping the dreamscape." Accessed April 1, 2023. https://medium.com/@gilan/mapping-the-dreamscape-cfb0a25859c

Healthline. "Lucid dreaming: Techniques, benefits, and cautions." Accessed April 1, 2023. https://www.healthline.com/health/healthy-sleep/how-to-lucid-dream

PRFC. "Healthy sleep habits for a restful night." Accessed April 1, 2023. https://prfc.me/health/healthy-sleep-habits-for-a-restful-night

Sleep Foundation. "How to interpret your dreams." Accessed April 1, 2023. https://www.sleepfoundation.org/dreams/dream-interpretation

Oniri. "How to stabilize a lucid dream." Accessed April 1, 2023. https://www.oniri.io/post/how-to-stabilize-a-lucid-dream

LEGO Dreamzzz. "How to talk to your kids about dreams." Accessed April 1, 2023. https://www.lego.com/en-us/themes/dreamzzz/talking-about-dreams

Oniri. "How to use meditation for lucid dreaming – A guide." Accessed April 1, 2023. https://www.oniri.io/post/meditation-for-lucid-dreaming

LonerWolf. "Hypnagogia: The trippy mental state that is the key to deep creativity." Accessed April 1, 2023. https://lonerwolf.com/hypnagogia

Phoenix Australia. "Imagery rehearsal manual." Accessed April 1, 2023. https://www.phoenixaustralia.org/disaster-hub/imagery-rehearsal-manual

PMC. "Investigation on neurobiological mechanisms of dreaming." Last modified 2021. https://pmc.ncbi.nlm.nih.gov/articles/PMC7916906

Jung, C. G. "The archetypes and the collective unconscious (Collected Works, Vol. 9, Part 1)." Princeton University Press, 1959

Northwestern Now. "Leveraging the power of lucid dreams." Last modified October 2024. https://news.northwestern.edu/stories/2024/10/leveraging-the-power-of-lucid-dreams

Mandala of Love. "The cross and the mandala." Last modified April 21, 2017. https://mandala-of-love.com/2017/04/21/cross-and-mandala

Maybe It's Just Me Blog. "The psychology of dreams: Common themes, theories and more." Last modified October 19, 2020. https://maybeitsjustme.blog/2020/10/19/the-psychology-of-dreams-common-themes-theories-and-more

The Lucid Guide. "Mnemonic induction of lucid dreaming (MILD)." Accessed April 1, 2023. https://www.thelucidguide.com/techniques/mnemonic-induction-of-lucid-dreaming-(mild)

Palmer, C. A., & Alfano, C. A. "Sleep and emotion regulation: An organizing, integrative review." Accessed April 1, 2023. https://doi.org/10.1016/j.smrv.2015.12.006

Psychology Today. "What's behind your recurring dreams?" Last modified November 1,

2014. https://www.psychologytoday.com/us/blog/dream-factory/201411/whats-behind-your-recurring-dreams

Psychology Today. "The link between mindfulness, meditation, and lucid dreaming." Last modified September 2015. https://www.psychologytoday.com/us/blog/dream-factory/201509/the-link-between-mindfulness-meditation-and-lucid-dreaming

Psychology Today. "The cultural dimensions of dreaming." Last modified April 2019. https://www.psychologytoday.com/us/blog/dreaming-in-the-digital-age/201904/the-cultural-dimensions-dreaming

Psychology Today. "The natural wisdom of children's dreams." Last modified May 2021. https://www.psychologytoday.com/us/blog/dreaming-in-the-digital-age/202105/the-natural-wisdom-childrens-dreams

PubMed. "REM sleep and memory." Last modified 2017. https://pubmed.ncbi.nlm.nih.gov/28544929

Sandler, P. "Commentary on 'Transformations in hallucinosis and the receptivity of the analyst' by Civitarese." Accessed April 1, 2023. https://doi.org/10.1111/1745-8315.12447

ScienceAlert. "The science of recurring dreams is more fascinating than we ever imagined." Accessed April 1, 2023. https://www.sciencealert.com/the-science-of-recurring-dreams-is-more-fascinating-than-we-ever-imagined

World of Lucid Dreaming. "Setting a lucid dream intention." Accessed April 1, 2023. https://www.world-of-lucid-dreaming.com/setting-a-lucid-dream-intention.html

Simply Psychology. "Sigmund Freud dream theory." Accessed April 1, 2023. https://www.simplypsychology.org/sigmund-freud-dream-theory.html

PMC. "The functional role of dreaming in emotional processes." Last modified 2019. https://pmc.ncbi.nlm.nih.gov/articles/PMC6428732

Vallat, R. "The science of dream recall." Accessed April 1, 2023. https://raphaelvallat.com/dreamrecall.html

Verywell Mind. "Why do we dream? Understanding dream theory." Accessed April 1, 2023. https://www.verywellmind.com/why-do-we-dream-top-dream-theories-2795931

Walker, M. P., & Stickgold, R. "Sleep, memory, and plasticity." Accessed April 1, 2023. https://doi.org/10.1146/annurev.psych.56.091103.070307

Sleep Foundation. "What is a dream journal used for?" Accessed April 1, 2023. https://www.sleepfoundation.org/dreams/dream-journal

Williams, L. A. "Assisting ministry leaders managing bipolar disorder in adolescents and young adults." Accessed April 1, 2023. https://core.ac.uk/download/595325442.pdf

www.ingramcontent.com/pod-product-compliance
Lightning Source LLC
Chambersburg PA
CBHW071731150426
43191CB00026B/1260